MOSES MENDELSSOHN

Moses Mendelssohn

Sage of Modernity

◆▬◆▬◆

SHMUEL FEINER

Translated from the Hebrew
by Anthony Berris

Yale
UNIVERSITY
PRESS

New Haven and London

Frontispiece: A fictitious meeting of, from left, Moses Mendelssohn, Gotthold Ephraim Lessing, and Johann Caspar Lavater; engraving after a painting by Moritz Daniel Oppenheim, 1856. akg-images.

Set in Janson Oldstyle type by Tseng Information Systems, Inc.
Printed in the United States of America.

Library of Congress Cataloging-in-Publication Data
Feiner, Shmuel.
[Mosheh Mendelson. English]
Moses Mendelssohn : sage of modernity / Shmuel Feiner ;
translated from the Hebrew by Anthony Berris.
p. cm. — (Jewish lives)
Includes bibliographical references and index.
ISBN 978-0-300-16175-5 (cloth : alk. paper) 1. Mendelssohn, Moses,
1729–1786. 2. Philosophers—Germany—Berlin—Biography.
3. Jews—Germany—Berlin—Biography. I. Title.
B2693.F4513 2010
193—dc22
[B]   2010020778

A catalogue record for this book is available from the British Library.

This paper meets the requirements of ANSI/NISO Z39.48-1992
(Permanence of Paper).

10 9 8 7 6 5 4 3 2 1

You must surely know what small part the members
of my faith have in all the freedoms of this country. The civic
oppression to which we are subject due to deep-rooted
prejudice lies like a deadweight on the wings of the spirit
and prevents any attempt to fly to the heights attained
by those who were born free.
—Moses Mendelssohn, 1762

I shall not deny that in my religion I have discerned
additions and distortions made by Man which, alas, dull its
splendor. What lover of truth can pride himself in that he
found his entire religion pure of harmful man-made laws? We
all seek the truth, we know the deleterious folly of hypocrisy
and superstition, and hope we shall possess the ability to rid
ourselves of it without damage to the true and the good.
But I am truly convinced that the essence of my
religion is immovable.
—Moses Mendelssohn, 1770

CONTENTS

1

A Stroll Down Unter den Linden

IN THE early evenings and on Sundays and holidays during the eighteenth century, many Berliners would take a pleasant stroll through the hunting grounds of the Tiergarten and down the linden-lined boulevard of Unter den Linden, which led to the royal palace. In the last decades of the century, the residents of the capital of the Kingdom of Prussia and numerous visitors to the city—who came to gain a firsthand impression of one of Europe's nascent cities of culture—could see Jews mingling with the other strollers in the city's parks and along its boulevards. The presence of many members of Berlin's Jewish community, which numbered some three thousand souls, in public places and in cultural sites—particularly theaters and concert halls—was characteristic of life in the vibrant city. Wealthy Jews, successful merchants and entrepreneurs, promenaded with their wives and daughters in fashionable attire, elegant coiffures, and ostentatious wigs, their fluent German and their refined manners worthy of the cultured bourgeoisie. Many of them read belles lettres and journals in various spheres of science and attended lectures on innovations in science and philosophy as well as cultural and artistic events. Notable among them were the physician and philosopher Marcus Herz, a disciple of Immanuel Kant, and Markus Bloch, the physician and scientist specializing in marine life, who were considered distinguished scholars and sources of pride for the city's residents.

On a summer evening in 1780, the city's most famous Jew, the eminent philosopher Moses Mendelssohn, was strolling through the city's streets with his wife, Fromet, and several of their children. A gang of youths began taunting the family with rhythmic, goading chanting of "*Juden! Juden!*" and threw stones at them. "What have we done to them, Father? Why do they always chase and curse us?" his shaken children asked. At that moment their father—upset, frustrated, and helpless—was unable to find comforting words and only murmured to himself with suppressed anger, "People, people, when will you stop this?"

Mendelssohn was by nature a reserved man. He never publicly expressed his feelings about the humiliating and terrifying experience undergone by his family. Only in one private letter to Peter Adolph Winkopp, a young Benedictine monk who was one of his most fervent admirers, did he write candidly about the incident. The episode was unusual but not unprecedented, and it cracked the veneer of Mendelssohn's respectability, damaged his self-respect, and shook his faith in his most treasured value, for which he had fought since becoming an important public figure in the intellectual world—religious tolerance. The country in which I live is allegedly a tolerant one, he wrote bitterly to Winkopp, but in fact I live in it under great stress, and the lack of tolerance assails me from all directions. What should I do? Perhaps lock up my children with me all day long at the silk factory where I work, just as you voluntarily imprison yourself in the monastery? Perhaps in this way I shall be able to spare them such cruel experiences? With cynicism tinged with despair and a sense of fatalism, he added: The situation certainly does not stimulate the literary and philosophical muses of the intellectual. Then, as if regretting such rare candor, he quickly sealed the window he had opened onto his feelings of affront and his existential situation as a Jew in Berlin. He reassured his Christian friend (and himself): Enough of these troubling thoughts! They only have a bad effect on my spirits and annoy me far too much. It would be better, Winkopp my friend, if I addressed the questions you asked about my philosophical book *Phädon* and not the frustrating and unresolved question of prejudice against the Jews. It would be better if I discussed with you the immortality of the soul, for that is a subject of great existential interest to all people, not only Jews. Mendelssohn never mentioned the street incident again.

Some six years later, on January 4, 1786, at 7 A.M. on a particularly cold winter morning in Berlin, Mendelssohn died in his home at 68 Spandau Street. He died young, four months after celebrating his fifty-sixth birthday with friends. Beginning at ten o'clock the next morning his coffin was borne through the streets of the center of Berlin to the old Jewish cemetery in Grosse Hamburger Street. Present at the well-attended funeral were his family, friends, and colleagues, including a large number of Christians, the leaders of the Berlin Jewish community, and members of the wealthy elite. Intellectuals, Jewish and Christian alike, felt a profound loss. On the day of the funeral, shops and businesses in Berlin were closed as a mark of respect. Nearly a thousand people crowded into the small cemetery.

Press coverage was extensive. Newspaper accounts of the great philosopher's death included detailed medical descriptions of his fatal illness. His personal physician, Dr. Marcus Herz, told readers about Mendelssohn's deteriorating condition and final hours. The Austrian ambassador to Berlin sent a message to his foreign minister in Vienna: "The renowned Jewish scholar Moses Mendelssohn died of a stroke yesterday." The eulogies were boundless. The maskilim, Jewish enlighteners, expressed their deep sorrow on the loss of an exemplary figure. They likened Mendelssohn to the biblical Moses and lamented his passing in biblical language: "Moses the man who raised us up from the mire, from the depths of ignorance to the halls of wisdom and knowledge, has left us." They sought solace in his spiritual legacy: "He will still speak to us of knowledge, not in words but in spirit, for among the wise of Israel he is unparalleled in his generation as a man so perfect of attributes and merit."

His Christian friends reacted emotionally to his sudden death in personal letters and newspaper articles. All agreed that Mendelssohn had been one of the leading lights of German philosophy and literature. He was a scholar of stature who had fought for truth, they wrote, and a man of exemplary virtue. They quoted his humanistic aphorisms, the watchwords addressed as salutations and dedications to his friends: "Strive for truth, love beauty, seek good, and do your best," "The world without love is chaos," "Love truth and peace." The eulogies were all but unanimous: not only thinkers and scholars but all citizens had lost a luminary, a symbol of hope for amity among men, and the prophet of the long-awaited day on which Jews and Christians would live as brothers. A few days after his death his admirers began planning commemorative projects. They began to raise funds, for example, to include Mendelssohn's portrait on a planned pyramidal monument honoring the great German scholars—Gottfried Wilhelm Leibniz, Johann Heinrich Lambert, and Johann Georg Sulzer—to be erected in Berlin's Opera Square.

Given the history of the Jews in Europe, this was an unprecedented event—Christian public opinion had never before so mourned a Jew. But Mendelssohn's fame in death mirrored his acclaim during the last two decades of his life as a brilliant thinker and scholar—"the German Socrates." Although he had not come from the same social circles as the German intellectuals, had not studied at the prestigious universities, had not, like many of his Christian friends, filled even a junior post in the government bureaucracy, and had not been a university lecturer or gymnasium teacher, he was acknowledged as one of the outstanding philosophers of the German Enlightenment.

The acute tension between these two stories—the dark, repressed tale of a humiliating anti-Jewish attack on Mendelssohn and his family on the streets of Berlin, the widely reported public account of the death of a giant of the German intellectual world—amplifies our fascination with the life and work of the world's most famous Jew in the eighteenth century. Mendelssohn was a historical sensation, and his Jewish and Christian contemporaries alike earmarked him as the man who could lead the Jewish transition from the old world of the "ghetto"—of cultural and social isolation—to the new world of Europe, to social and cultural integration, the weakening of the traditional commitment to religion and community.

After his death Mendelssohn's reputation took on mythical proportions. This stocky man, thick-browed and brown-eyed, with black hair, a sparse beard, and a pronounced curvature of the spine, became the symbol of Jewish modernism. The life story of the Dessau-born scholar, who made a living from clerical work in a silk factory, was known throughout Europe. In intellectual circles he represented the ideal of the self-created man who overcame physical disabilities and a sometimes hostile environment by dint of intellect and character, and blazed his way to fame. He succeeded in shattering the existential framework into which he was born and resolutely building an international career, thereby gaining international status. His belonging to Jewish society, a people marginalized in European culture for centuries, only enhanced the myth of the Enlightenment hero, thriving against all odds.

Many from Mendelssohn's generation knew his face from numerous portraits that were painted from his mid-thirties until shortly before his death. His likeness was fired on porcelain teacups and tableware, it appeared on vases and pendants and in colored pictures, engravings, and busts that were fashioned in his lifetime, helping to turn him into a cultural hero, a "brand." Mendelssohn's silhouette even appeared in the pseudo-scientific and controversial book on physiognomy by Johann Caspar Lavater, a Swiss pastor who played a decisive role in Mendelssohn's life when he forced him into a complex and embarrassing public debate. Lavater enthusiastically examined Mendelssohn's features, which, in the opinion of the physiognomist, reflected his attributes: "My glance descends from the noble curve of the forehead to the prominent bones of the eye. In the depth of this eye a Socratic soul resides. The decided shape of the nose, the magnificent transition from the nose to the upper lip, the prominence of both lips, neither projecting beyond the other, oh, how all this harmonizes and makes the divine truth of physiognomy sensible and visible." In this son of Abraham, Lavater concluded, were merged Plato and the Biblical Moses.

The eighteenth century, said Samuel Johnson, the distinguished British author, editor, and critic and a contemporary of Mendelssohn, was "the era of authors." With the proliferation of literacy in Europe, Latin—the language of scholars, known only to a small, exclusive group—was further marginalized and largely supplanted in publication by vernacular languages. As book markets expanded, the place of theological works and books of religious ritual was increasingly usurped by novels, travel journals, and volumes of history, science, philosophy, and poetry. Scholars of reading culture write about "the passion for reading" during this period, and about a subsequent "reading revolution." Daily newspapers and other periodicals circulated widely, reading clubs and lending libraries flourished, and writers' prestige was high. This was particularly notable in the German-speaking countries, where the number of writers grew from 4,300 in 1776 to 5,200 in 1784 to 7,000 in 1791. Only a few (perhaps 2 percent) made a living from writing; most held state positions in universities and government bureaus. But their public influence increased considerably. The Hohenzollern dynast King Friedrich II ("The Great") of Prussia himself wrote philosophical essays, was involved in the Königliche Akademie der Wissenschaften (Royal Academy of Science), and cultivated intellectuals, philosophers, and authors. Multivolume biographies were published of contemporary authors, and their portraits hung in the homes of the wealthy and the bourgeoisie. Mendelssohn entered this exclusive cultural circle of German writers with philosophers of previous generations, like Leibniz and Christian Wolff, as well as such contemporary authors, poets, dramatists, and philosophers as Gotthold Ephraim Lessing, Christian Gellert, Friedrich Gottlieb Klopstock, Christoph Martin Wieland, Immanuel Kant, Johann Gottfried Herder, Johann Wolfgang von Goethe, and many others. This was an unprecedented achievement for a Jew, and everyone in the writing community of Mendelssohn's generation took note. The Protestant preacher Daniel Jenisch, for instance, viewed him as the Jewish Martin Luther. His book *Phädon*, in which he argues for the immortality of the soul, was a spectacular success, credited by many as consoling countless readers with reasoned evidence that death is not absolute oblivion but a reward for which mankind should yearn. After his own death, pictures were published and allegorical plays staged in which he was portrayed as dwelling in the next world with the titans of both Western and Jewish culture: Socrates, Moses, Maimonides. In one hagiographical picture Mendelssohn is borne to heaven after his death and welcomed by the Almighty and his angels.

In the historical accounts of German-Jewish historians, Mendelssohn represents the beginning of the new era in Jewish history, the public ideal for modern Jews. His curriculum vitae was meticulously reconstructed, his writings and hundreds of letters in Hebrew and German were collected, and a vast enterprise of publishing his collected works—meant to mark the bicentennial of his birth—began in the mid-twentieth century, only to be cut short by the Holocaust. His place as the father of the Jewish Enlightenment Movement, and as an exemplary figure in the history of German Jewry and of the entire Jewish people, was ensured for generations to come. Special emphasis was placed on his role as the harbinger of the emancipation of European Jews: liberation from discrimination and restrictions, equality in human rights. Mendelssohn was perceived as the embodiment of the great historic defining moment in Jewish-Christian relations. His close friendship with the author and dramatist Lessing was presented as an exemplar for the future, a symbol of social and legal equality for Jews,—equality withheld in fact from the Jews of Germany for almost a century after his death. More particularly, this friendship reflected the beginning of a process of moderate integration—social integration that did not deny the legitimacy of Jewish solidarity, did not insist upon assimilation—for Mendelssohn knew how to fend off any attempt to lead him to Christianity.

Heinrich Graetz, for example, one of the nineteenth century's most important historians and a great admirer of Mendelssohn, described the philosopher's period in Jewish history in enthusiastic and messianic terms of Jewish renaissance, during which latent talents emerged and a new Jewish era became possible. The life story of this exemplary and unblemished figure, Graetz contended, embodies the essence of the entire

Jewish history in the Modern Era, especially the hope of emergence from the "darkness" of the Middle Ages. For Graetz, Mendelssohn was a cultural hero of titanic proportions, and in the scholarly writing of Graetz and others, Mendelssohn's figure dominates the collective memory of German Jewry. Mendelssohn was a Jew with whom one could easily identify, a Jew who brought honor to Judaism, who proved that a Jew of the New Era could be a loyal German citizen and at home in German culture and language, and still be connected to his Jewish community and cultural heritage. Mendelssohn was the prototype of German Jewry in the era of legal emancipation and social integration into the bourgeoisie, and he provided a sort of respectful entrée into state and society. For German Jewry, which for years had repeatedly to prove its acceptability, its worthiness to exist alongside the majority, to blend in, the historical Mendelssohn was a valuable asset, the ideal representative of those who dreamed of symbiosis between Jewish and Christian Germans.

However, as the myth of Mendelssohn the reconciler waxed, the conservative camp of modern Jewish society crafted a countermyth. Even as Jewish conservatism was gradually splitting, its adherents rejected the transformation in the destiny of the Jews associated with the historical Mendelssohn; conservatives repudiated the need to break out of the confines of traditional Jewish-religious life in the community. They anxiously witnessed the processes of modernization and forecast a systemic collapse. Growing interest in the spheres of nonreligious knowledge, especially philosophy, seemed to them the gateway to apostasy. They mythologized Mendelssohn accordingly. To them he became a demonic historical figure possessed of destructive forces and responsible for all the crises of the Modern Era: assimilation, disintegration of the traditional community, loss of faith, religious permissiveness, and erosion of the authority of the rabbinical elite. Against the narrative favored by enlightened and liberal Jewry, they told of a wicked plot for a vast and malicious revolt against tradition and the rabbis. Rabbi Akiva Joseph Schlesinger, a disciple of Rabbi Moses Sofer (the Chatam Sofer) known as one of the fathers of the Orthodox resistance to the modern trends in Judaism, perceived Mendelssohn as a leader of the revolt against the Jewish religion: "The evil Moses of Dessau, the leader of the rebels who has the cunning of a snake . . . has begun bringing the foreign harlot among the Jews to make them go whoring after false gods, which is to say, worshiping other gods."

In fact, Mendelssohn's eulogizers and detractors viewed the historical figure much the same—myth and countermyth alike accorded him the proportions of a giant possessing tremendous ability to drive the wheels of Jewish history. Each camp presented Mendelssohn one-dimensionally—as a historical cultural hero on the one hand, as a demon, "the leader of the rebels," on the other. For better or worse they labeled him as the man who had driven all the New Era's processes of change—education, religious reform, secularization, assimilation, integration—all the forces of modernization undergone by the Jews over the past three hundred years.

Nor was this an ex nihilo creation, for even decades after his death the creators of the Mendelssohnian myth still employed the foundations laid by Mendelssohn's contemporaries, Jews and Christians who perceived him as an unparalleled historical sensation. In later generations the historical Mendelssohn became a pawn to the partisans of various agendas, each waving him like a banner and adopting him for its particular worldview. Some flaunted him to prove the merits of Jewish modernism and cultural and social openness, whereas others did the same to prove the opposite. Contemporary historians, however, have explored the complexity of Jewish modernization and the numerous channels of change. In many Jewish communities in the West, those of Amsterdam and London for example, the foundations of modern modes of life predated Mendelssohn's contributions by decades. In contrast, in many communities in eastern Europe and the Islamic countries the traditional modes began to change only in the final decades of the nineteenth century, and in historical, political, economic, and cultural contexts that had nothing to do with Mendelssohn. Today, any approach that ascribes credit (or blame) for the entire gamut of modernization processes to one man—no matter how great his stature—seems naïve and simplistic.

This biography is not meant to further the portrayal of Mendelssohn as a symbol, a paragon, or a leader who led a historical process of vast proportions. My aim, rather, is to present him neither as hero nor as antihero but as the intriguing, complex, fascinating man he was: the eminent Jewish philosopher who in the second half of the eighteenth century attained a public status unprecedented for a Jew. But literary exposure and renown came with a price. All his life Mendelssohn aspired to contribute in his writing to the philosophical discourse of his time while at the same time distancing himself from the public milieu enough to preserve his private life—in the parlor, the study, the family, the community, the silk factory, and the synagogue. Once he chose the life of a Jewish intellectual involved in the community of European men of culture, though, Mendelssohn found himself, time and again, propelled to the center of the public stage. Public opinion—inquisitive, interested, admiring, or critical—was inescapable. The social circles to which he belonged were the shapers of culture and the ideological world. It soon became clear to him that he was under scrutiny and that his celebrity in the public sphere was also projected onto the Jewish society. On the one hand, the communities' leaders basked in the honor bestowed on him, and now and again tried to enlist him to act on behalf of the interests of the

Jews; on the other, his status as an unconventional creator of culture in contemporary Judaism placed him constantly under suspicion of the rabbinical elite.

Mendelssohn found himself competing with colleagues and adversaries, Jews and Gentiles alike. He was among the first Jewish philosophers compelled to deal directly with the challenges of "the modern Jewish situation." He had both to formulate his own values in the thorny encounter between traditional Jewish culture and the values of European enlightenment and to resolve dilemmas that emerged as a consequence of this encounter. Furthermore, he had to defend his values in the face of public criticism leveled at him from various directions—from non-Jewish intellectuals and clerics striving to comprehend the historical impact of this Moses of Dessau, and from rabbis protective of their own status and authority. In "the modern Jewish situation" in which Mendelssohn found himself, these dilemmas, perplexities, contradictions, and challenges were manifest not only in the closed circles of the Jewish community or the synagogues, and not only in the religious language and texts restricted solely to Jews, but in public opinion, as embodied in the daily papers, journals, scholars' reading clubs, cafés, literary salons, and the extensive correspondence network of which Mendelssohn was part. Mendelssohn's unprecedented visibility mandated that he be extremely circumspect; it often frustrated him, led him to fight for his values when they were put to the test, and sometimes—as in the street incident suffered by his family—to minimize events that ran so depressingly counter to Enlightenment ideals.

The tests Mendelssohn faced in the public sphere were those of the Enlightenment. The term *Enlightenment* refers to a trend in eighteenth-century Western culture toward belief in humanistic values, religious tolerance, the right of humankind to freedom and happiness, and the ability of human society to improve itself, to adopt a more humanitarian way of life. The

Enlightenment in central and western Europe was not monolithic. It comprised a variety of attitudes, a variety of intellectuals, and a variety of agendas and programs pursued in a variety
of places. The French Enlightenment, for instance, was characterized by harsh criticism of the church, and in certain quarters
by political subversion. The German Enlightenment, on the
other hand, was relatively moderate, generally adhering to Protestantism or Catholicism. Eschewing radical political criticism,
the German movement sought to attract the educated citizen,
and its numbers included such representatives of the establishment as officials, academics, teachers, and clerics. All, however,
were united around the Enlightenment project—reformation
of society through the power of reason and the belief in natural
rights, education, appropriate laws, and responsible rulers. The
project might be called salvation through knowledge—knowledge whose dissemination would make people happier, more
aware of their world, more moral and independent.

The Enlightenment project's principal success was in
placing the modern intellectuals involved in society at the center. It was the enlightened who in a significant revolutionary
step created the public sphere—a sphere of discourse, com-
munication, and exchange of knowledge, ideas, and opinions
through the printed word. It was they who invented critical "public opinion," which scrutinized public life and which
judged ideas and deeds. It was they who in the eighteenth century imbued people's consciousness with the basic concepts and
images of the changing times, of the chance of progress, and
of the promising horizons for a humankind awakening from
cultural hibernation and intellectual stagnation. Mendelssohn
was a fully fledged member of the Enlightenment culture of his
time, and as we shall see, also one of its architects.

For the Jews of Europe the Enlightenment also introduced
into public discourse "the Jewish Question"—the debate on
how the Jews would take part, if at all, in the New Era. If up to

that point Christian theological thinking had formed the ideological basis of European society's engagement with the Jews
and Judaism, the flourishing of Enlightenment culture raised a
series of new questions that were secular in nature: what kind
of relations should exist between the Jews and the state? Should
their right be preserved to organize in the framework of an autonomous Jewish community? Should Jewish religious leaders
retain the authority to impose the precepts of Jewish law?
How should they be educated, what would their identity be,
in which occupations would they engage, what language would
they speak, what clothing would they wear, and how would they
spend their leisure? Among the enlightened—the most notable
of whom was Voltaire—some held the character of the Jews to
be so corrupt that they were beyond redemption. In the view of
such observers, even general secular relations, free of the false
accusations of Christian theologians, would of necessity leave
the Jews as a discrete group, separate from civil society. Others,
though, drew from the universal values of the Enlightenment
to conclude that humankind was humankind, regardless of historical, religious, and ethnic affiliation. According to them, the
principles of religious tolerance must be adopted, freeing the
Jews from anachronistic restrictions that had been the product
of prejudices of a dark era.

The rules of the game changed drastically from the moment when Enlightenment thinkers secularized thinking on
Jewish-Christian relations and minimized the groups' theological rivalry. Secular discourse, however, posed a new challenge to the Jewish society. Jewish intellectuals favored assimilation of Enlightenment values as a route to revolution in the
destiny of European Jewry. Throughout the eighteenth century, particularly its last quarter, they had cited the need to
embrace enlightenment and religious tolerance, and to support
political regimes that applied a policy of tolerance, especially
Austria of the 1780s under Emperor Josef II. On the other

hand, some conservative rabbis feared that the Enlightenment, with its rationalistic philosophy and modern education, would undermine religious tradition

This struggle between the Jewish Enlightenment intellectuals and Orthodox resistance complicated Jewish life. For many Jews the Enlightenment provided hope for a long-imagined freedom. But with new hope, of course, came a new possibility for bitter disappointment. The borders between "us" and "the others" created by religious and community worldviews had been extremely clear. Jews had lived by prophecies of divine redemption from exile and other tidings of the End of Days. The Enlightenment brought a different sort of redemption. Mendelssohn was no naïve optimist, but he was among those Jews who hoped that the culture of the Enlightenment would enable them to live a more dignified life and free them from humiliating restrictions. He was thus particularly sensitive to the fluctuations of public opinion toward the Jews; failures in fulfillment of Enlightenment values haunted him to his dying day.

Thus we study Moses Mendelssohn not only to reconstruct the principal benchmarks in his life, or to discuss the essentials of his philosophical thinking, but also to reveal the dilemmas inherent in the Jews' experience of modernity. To scrutinize Mendelssohn's soul is to discover a tragic tension between, on one hand, the Enlightenment's liberal fighter, who took aim against religious fanaticism, political oppression, and superstition in the name of reason, morality, and humanism, and, on the other hand, the sensitive, vulnerable man who felt helpless in the face of the invincible forces of what he called "the specters of the dead." It is to see, on an existential plane, the tension between the philosopher who was a household name, able to cross the borders of "otherness" into non-Jewish circles, and the Berlin Jew who felt oppressed in the Prussia of Friedrich II. The lens of humanism through which Mendelssohn examined human reality only magnified the "otherness" of his

Jewish affiliation. This contradiction aroused in Mendelssohn a bitter dread that the Enlightenment had failed.

The vast quantity of documentation, especially Mendelssohn's writings and correspondence, affords us a window into the hopes, distresses, and disappointments of one of the master builders of German Enlightenment culture, who was at the same time one of the renewers of Jewish culture in Europe. In a modernist experience that incorporated both reconciliation of the humanistic values of the Enlightenment with the Jewish minority and liberation of Jewish culture from the hegemony of the rabbinic elite, Mendelssohn repeatedly tested Enlightenment colleagues, Jewish compatriots, and himself. To begin our inquiry, however, we must first go back to the early stages of his life, to discover how the decisive transformation took place—how a talented youth destined to join the elite of rabbinical scholars became a renowned Jewish-German philosopher.

2

From Dessau to Berlin:
An Unpredicted Career

IN THE spring of 1761, when Moses Mendelssohn was
thirty-two, he traveled to northern Germany to visit the home
of Rabbi Jonathan Eybeschütz, one of Ashkenazi Jewry's greatest rabbis. It seems that Mendelssohn, in view of his Talmudic
erudition, expected Eybeschütz to grant him the rabbinic title
morenu, "our teacher," or the somewhat inferior *haver,* "peer."
Eybeschütz possessed this power by virtue of his authority as
the community rabbi of Altona as well as the neighboring Hamburg and Wandsbek. In the 1750s Eybeschütz was accused by
his bitter adversary, Rabbi Jacob Emden, of secretly believing
in the messianic pretender Shabetai Zevi. Emden claimed that
Eybeschütz was giving women amulets of Sabbatean content
that were supposed to safeguard them during childbirth. But
Emden's charges could not detract from Eybeschütz's prestige
as one of the senior members of the rabbinic elite. What tran-
spired at his meeting with Mendelssohn is unknown, but there

is no doubt that Mendelssohn impressed Rabbi Eybeschütz with his erudition. Eybeschütz tested him and was amazed by both his Talmudic erudition and his knowledge of science and philosophy. He likened Mendelssohn to his biblical namesake: "For Moses' hands are heavy and his ability great in learning and natural wisdom, research, logic, philosophy, and rhetoric."

But the meeting in Altona did not yield rabbinic ordination. Eybeschütz apparently found himself torn: could he grant the title of rabbi to a Jewish philosopher who wrote in German in the literary journals of German intellectuals? Would it be appropriate to grant the title to a man who had, from the point of view of Jewish culture, taken an unprecedented step by crossing the border between Jew and Gentile? Could he give Mendelssohn a membership card that would identify him in the general public arena and also as a member of the rabbinic elite? In the end Eybeschütz decided that a letter of recommendation replete with praise would suffice, thus sidestepping formal ordination to the rabbinate. Granting the title of *haver*, Rabbi Eybeschütz explained in his rejection, would constitute diminished respect for a Jew of Mendelssohn's stature; because he was still unmarried, on the other hand, he could not be ordained *morenu*, which would enable him to rule on matters of Jewish law. Therefore, Eybeschütz wrote, all he could grant Mendelssohn was his blessing and "a covering of the eyes" (after Genesis, 20:16), a kind of testimonial to his visitor's legitimacy as a scholar.

Rabbi Eybeschütz seems to have been conscious at this meeting of the significance of the transformation undergone by the young Mendelssohn; by denying this individualist membership in the religious elite he may have meant to preserve the uniformity of the group of rabbis, to safeguard its borders. Whatever Eybeschütz's motives, his resistance had long-term implications whose importance cannot be overstated. From that time on, Mendelssohn's Jewish philosophical and literary activities took place outside the rabbinic milieu. He became the unquestioned representative of a nonrabbinical Jewish intellectual elite that could operate in the milieu of modern secular philosophy and literature.

Mendelssohn's deviation from his preordained career as a Torah scholar had an undeniably decisive impact on his life. Until his twenties at least, the life of the talented boy from Dessau moved along the accepted training track for the career of a great Torah scholar. The only respected career for the intellectual elite in premodern Jewish society was in the rabbinic elite. Rabbi Eybeschütz, for instance, believed that other rabbis before him had granted Mendelssohn the title of *haver*, which was usually given to a talented yeshiva student at about twenty years of age. Mendelssohn began in his twenties, however, to take a different path—toward the unconventional career of a German-Jewish philosopher and writer in enlightened Berlin. Mendelssohn moved as a Jew from the outside, from the periphery invisible to the general public, from the exclusive sphere of the closed knowledge of the Jews, into the arena of secular, cultural, and philosophical discourse of Europe. How did this extraordinary change take place? To answer that question, we must examine Mendelssohn's youth and adolescence.

Moses, the son of Menachem (Mendel), a Torah scribe, and Bella Rachel Sarah, was born at No. 10 Spitalgasse in Dessau, capital of the principality of Anhalt-Dessau, on September 6, 1729. The community into which he was born was typical of eighteenth-century German Jewry: a relatively small community of merchants founded at the end of the seventeenth century and numbering only a few hundred Jews. The main Jewish centers of the time were in Poland and Lithuania, where hundreds of thousands of Jews lived. Germany in the period following the brutal and prolonged internecine wars between Protestants and Catholics was far from a unified political entity. It constituted a loose geographical, linguistic, and cultural framework that was officially called the Holy Roman Empire of the German Nation and comprised more than three hundred independent political entities. Dispersed throughout these states in the early years of Mendelssohn's life were numerous small Jewish communities, whose total population numbered seventy thousand at most. In the eighteenth century the German states, badly damaged during the internecine wars, undertook a reconstruction process. The absolutist system employed by many rulers supported centralization—the central government was given sweeping authority for everything taking place in its territory. In principle nothing changed in the class division of the society, and concepts such as "liberty" and "equality" remained in the purview of the intellectuals. However, the raison d'état was that the state could be a source of welfare for the population contributed to rationalization of government and of the bureaucracy, and toward reform of law, justice, administration, the economy, and the army.

These changes inevitably affected Jews in the German states. Opportunity for economic initiative expanded for affluent Jews, who were quick to take advantage. In absolutist states not only did the well-to-do dictate the movement of capital and goods, some became "court Jews"—advisers to kings and princes, who helped to build the state and its economic and military systems. This elite also used its newfound wealth to develop the Jewish communities. Court Jews and entrepreneurs were given special permits to live where no Jewish community existed, and to establish such community institutions as cemeteries and synagogues. Although critics decried the oligarchic character of the wealthy elite, these wealthy Jews provided the foundations and the leadership of many Jewish communities in Germany. So it was with the Dessau community, where a decisive developmental role was played by Moses Benjamin Wulff, who bore the title of *Hoffaktor*, court administrator. Due to their daily contact with the Christian aristocratic ruling elite, and their eagerness to flaunt their economic status through displays of wealth, the members of this elite were among the first German Jews to adopt a European lifestyle and culture, including the language of the country in which they lived. Still, until the end of the eighteenth century most of them continued to identify and be identified with Jewish life: the autonomous community with its institutions, religious culture, and traditions. These wealthy Jews invested substantial sums of money in Jewish institutions, becoming the patrons of the religious elite. Thus, for example, among Benjamin Wulff's properties were a Hebrew printing press and a *beit midrash*, a religious academy for advanced Talmudic and Jewish law studies, which was run under his aegis and at his expense.

The Mendelssohn family was not among the wealthy elite, even though Moses's mother, Sarah, was a cousin of Eliahu Wulff, one of the community's leaders and son and heir of Moses Benjamin Wulff. Moses's father, Menachem, was the synagogue treasurer, Torah scribe, and teacher, an occupation on a lower rung of the social ladder. Mendelssohn remained conscious of his class inferiority throughout his life, and even at the peak of his success he did not perceive himself part of the Jewish aristocracy. Yet as a child he possessed all the resources necessary to pursue a career in religion—inquisitiveness, talent, pedigree, and the encouragement in the value of Torah study of those around him. His scholarly talents were revealed during his years in the *heder*, where the ability to understand the knotty questions in the Talmud was the principal yardstick of selection for the few who would continue with advanced studies in a yeshiva. There was no alternative career track in the traditional education system. A scholar, as defined by the Jewish community, studied Talmud and religious law on his own, and no other academic course existed. Religion determined values, way of life, and worldview, and this was manifested in Jewish society by Torah study and religious observance.

As in the majority of premodern Jewish communities, in Dessau in the 1730s the family, the community, and the rabbinic leadership cultivated an elite of Torah scholars. Mendelssohn's family was proud of its kinship with a prestigious rabbinic dynasty. His mother came from a family of rabbis and wealthy landowners from Poland; her most illustrious forebear was Rabbi Moses Isserles of Cracow, the great sixteenth-century Ashkenazi Talmudist. Apart from wealth, leadership status in the community, or membership in the rabbinate, pedigree was a mark of social class. Descent from Rabbi Isserles accorded great prestige and served to motivate young Moses to prepare to follow in the footsteps of the great Talmudic scholars of previous generations. Indeed, we can reasonably assume that his parents named him Moses after both the highly esteemed court Jew of Dessau and Rabbi Isserles.

There can be no doubt, however, that the key role in preparing Moses, son of Menachem, to join the ranks of the rabbinical elite was played by Rabbi David Fränkel, who was described by Alexander Altmann, Mendelssohn's most prominent biographer, as a father figure in young Moses's life. Almost no information exists about Mendelssohn's relationship with his father, who, it may be assumed, played only a minor role in his training. Menachem was a relatively old man of forty-seven when Moses was born, and he was viewed by his son as "a man of the old world." At the time, the training of Torah scholars was undertaken by rabbis of stature who also took upon themselves the running of a local yeshiva. Rabbi Fränkel, the rabbi of Dessau beginning in 1731, devoted himself to his community roles. He displayed particular creativity in his unconventional occupation with the Jerusalem Talmud (on which he wrote the important commentary *Korban Ha'edah*); incorporated the writings of Maimonides into Torah study by printing a new edition of his magnum opus on Jewish law, *Mishneh Torah* (1739); gained the support of the wealthy elite; and fostered young students. When Mendelssohn was eleven, he joined the yeshiva run by Rabbi Fränkel in his house, where some thirty boys studied the Talmud and the *Shulchan Aruch*, the codification of Jewish law.

The first preserved text written by Mendelssohn was composed in the rabbi's house one month before the student's thirteenth birthday and attests to his youthful aspirations. In the summer of 1742 Mendelssohn wrote several lines in praise of his revered rabbi in a volume of the responsa of Rabbi Isaac Ben Sheshet (the Rivash), *She'elot Uteshuvot HaRivash:*

> Inscribed in the house of the superior and eminent rabbi, the *Gaon*, our crown, the paragon of beauty, the diadem of holiness, lover of Israel, the magnificent of our generation, the great scholar, his reverence our master and teacher Rabbi David, may his light shine, author of the commentary and annotations to the Jerusalem Talmud, may the Almighty grant him and all who dwell in his shadow long life until the Messiah comes, head of the rabbinical court and head of the yeshiva here in the holy community of Dessau.

The boy's fluency in florid rabbinical language peppered with its conventional rabbinic codes, as well as his great admiration for his rabbi, illustrates that even in his youth he was deeply immersed in the world of Torah scholars, with its ethos of Talmudic and Halachic scholarship, its specialized language, and the centrality of its rabbis. Had Mendelssohn's rabbinical career continued developing along the usual course, he would soon have earned all the titles extolling talmudic scholarship and displayed all the attributes that Jewish society admired as the pinnacle of intellectual achievement.

Mendelssohn took a significant step toward that pinnacle a year later. When he was fourteen he decided to leave his parents, his brother Joseph, and his sister Brendel in Dessau and go to Berlin, where, in the summer of 1743, Rabbi Fränkel was appointed chief rabbi. It was not uncommon in scholarly circles for a young Torah scholar to follow his rabbi and move with his Torah study center, but the move to Berlin was particularly significant for Mendelssohn. It was there, when he was in his twenties, that his career took the turn from Torah scholarship to philosophy.

A dramatic story is told of the thin, frail young man's walk from the city of his birth to Berlin, a distance of nearly ninety miles. In fact, he probably reached his destination by post coach, but the story of his confrontation with the Jewish guard at one of the city's gates is better documented: the guard refused to admit Mendelssohn until he was convinced that the traveler desired solely to study Torah. This episode illustrates the character of the life of Prussian Jews in the first decade of the reign of Friedrich the Great. Prussian absolutism was rigid, and the regime's ambition to impose order on its subjects had immediate implications for the Jewish communities of Prussia in general, and for that of Berlin in particular. On the one hand, the House of Hohenzollern and its officials were eager to develop the commercial and industrial potential of religious minorities, including the wealthy, entrepreneurial Jews. The state even granted Jews various concessions to spur the mercantile economy and encourage its salient principle of filling the state coffers. On the other hand, dating to 1671, when the Elector of Brandenburg, Friedrich Wilhelm I, had allowed Jews again to reside in Berlin, their numbers were rigidly limited, with the declared aim of reducing the overall Jewish population in the capital and restricting that population to only "useful" Jews and those who either served them or were necessary for the community's social and religious functioning.

The implications of this Prussian policy on the character of the Berlin community were severe. Some fifteen wealthy families, engaged mainly in commerce, banking, and the textile industry, were the backbone of the Jewish community. They constituted the Jewish aristocracy, whose sons and daughters intermarried. Occasionally nouveaux riches joined their ranks—people like Daniel Itzig and Veitel Heine Ephraim, whose families had great influence in Mendelssohn's time. The Prussian economy was tightly controlled. One manifestation of Prussian absolutism was a supervisory system over economic activities; the Jews fueled the economy with fees, taxes, and other payments in exchange for needed privileges, licenses, and concessions. In order to divest itself of Jews unbeneficial to the economic system, the state enlisted community leaders and officials to implement policy to that effect. Not only did community leaders have to report on fluctuations in the number of Jews, they were obliged to drive problematic intruders—vagabonds and hawkers, for example—from the city limits. This policy illustrates the close and complex connection among Prussian absolutism, the country's economic interests, the legal status of Jews, and class distinctions that helped shaped the character of the Jewish community in Berlin. But despite the harsh decrees and guards posted at the gates, the Jewish community grew beyond expectations, and in the 1740s it numbered some two thousand Jews. In their capacity as leaders of the community, wealthy men assumed supervisory roles without forfeiting their connection with the community and its values. In general the wealthy elite remained loyal to traditional values and ideals; late in the eighteenth century these community leaders still maintained the social status of Torah scholars and the rabbis, even though their own authority was in fact much stronger.

Legally, the fourteen-year-old boy just arrived from Dessau was an alien who could not present the necessary letter of protection (*Schutzbrief*), but once he was recognized as a Torah scholar—studying under the aegis of Rabbi Fränkel and given free lodging with one of the community's leading families (he was registered as a protégé of Chaim Bamberger)—Mendelssohn was able to stay in the city in relative security. In the mid-1740s his world was still demarcated by the Jewish environment—the streets and alleys of the Jewish residential area in the city center, the attic in the Bamberger house on Probstgasse where he lived, the home of the Jews who hosted him and other young Torah scholars for meals, the splendid synagogue at No. 4 Heidereutergasse that was founded in 1714, and the house of Rabbi David Fränkel adjoining the synagogue and the *beit midrash*. His intellectual world was bounded by the library of the learned elite, at the center of which stood the Talmud and its commentators, Halachic literature, together with popular books on ethics.

A change in this Jewish library, as well as Mendelssohn's friendship with three unconventional Jews during his adolescent years, began to nudge him from the course of a rabbinical career. A year before Mendelssohn's arrival in Berlin, Israel ben Abraham, a former Christian who had converted to Judaism and who owned the Hebrew printing house in Jessnitz near Dessau, printed Maimonides' influential book on philosophy *Moreh Nevukhim* (The guide for the perplexed). The book, which was written in the twelfth century and first printed in the sixteenth, had not been reprinted for some two hundred years. This neglect was no accident—medieval Jewish philosophy was the preserve of a few, while the ideas, concepts, and secrets of the Kabbalah were far more attractive than the rationalistic notions of philosophy. Some rabbis even upheld the fourteenth-century proscription against the study of philosophy as a threat to the integrity of religious belief. The restoration of *Moreh Nevukhim* to the Jewish library through its reprinting in 1742 exposed Mendelssohn to long-obscured ideas during the first years of his studies in Berlin. He studied the book closely, and from this early stage of his life until his dying day he admired and internalized Maimonides' intellectual ideal: that men capable of profound thought are obliged to aspire to perfection and recognize the truth and God by means of their intellect, in Maimonides' rendering of Jeremiah 9:23, "that he understandeth and knoweth me." Many years later Mendels-sohn attributed his physical weakness and the curvature of his spine to the great effort he invested in studying Maimonides. "He afflicted my flesh and I became feeble because of him," his first Jewish biographer Isaac Euchel quoted him, "and yet I loved him greatly for he transformed many hours in my life-time from sorrow into joy."

Thus, a twelfth-century philosophical text intended to pre-sent a Jewish religion free of superstition and of a personified deity inspired the novice Torah scholar to yearn for abstract ideas, truths, and clear and defined concepts—and ushered him toward philosophy. His entry into the world of medi-eval Jewish philosophy was facilitated by Israel Samoscz, who had come to Berlin from Galicia and had gained the patron-age of wealthy Jews as an extraordinary scholar. In 1744, at the same press in Jessnitz, Samoscz published *Ruach Chen* (Spirit of grace), a commentary on the philosophical lexicon attrib-uted to Judah Ibn Tibbon. Samoscz later wrote a commentary on the classical volumes of ethics and philosophy of the Span-ish Golden Age: the eleventh-century *Chovot Ha-Levavot* (In-struction in the duties of the heart) by Bahya Ibn Paquda, and Judah Halevi's twelfth-century *The Kuzari*. No one was more suitable than he to teach Jewish philosophy to Mendelssohn, who was some twenty years his junior. For Mendelssohn, Israel Samoscz was evidently far more than a personal tutor in the understanding of texts not taught in the religious schools of the time. His inclination toward science and philosophy was complemented by a comprehensive worldview. He was given to criticism of the limitations, restrictions, and barrenness of the religious culture whence he came. He was angered by the contempt in which Jewish scholars held "external wisdom"— the sciences and philosophy—but it would be erroneous to assume that Samoscz's aspiration to broaden the knowledge of the rabbinical elite derived from a desire to undermine the Jewish religion or the foundations of its beliefs. On the contrary, he believed that his criticism would bring about purification of that belief, improvement of religious scholarship, and eradication of ignorance. Throughout his life Israel Samoscz remained a member of the rabbinical elite, but he represented an eighteenth-century change that he managed to convey to Mendelssohn. The scholars who internalized this critical, reformist worldview belonged to the rabbinical elite but were disturbed by the Jews' cultural inferiority to the Christians and were dedicated to combating stupidity and ignorance; saving neglected Jewish texts on science, the Hebrew language, and philosophy; and learning "external wisdom." These men participated in the historical-cultural-social revolution in the makeup of the Jewish intellectual elite.

Mendelssohn and Samoscz were not the only ones in Berlin of the 1740s to play a part in this transformation. Abraham Kisch, a medical student from Prague, gave Mendelssohn Latin lessons, thus introducing him to the European scholarly library, unexplored by the vast majority of the rabbinic elite. A close personal friend, Aaron Gumpertz, was Mendelssohn's chief instructor during his adolescent years. Gumpertz was six years older than Mendelssohn, a son of one of the distinguished families of the economic elite, and a keen intellectual. Years after the death of this admired friend of his youth, Mendelssohn wrote that to Gumpertz alone he owed everything he had achieved in the sciences. Gumpertz developed Mendelssohn's propensity for science and philosophy and set before him the model of the knowledge-hungry intellectual. It was he who guided Mendelssohn along the road to the ultimate ideal of scholar and philosopher: together they encountered the writings of Christian scholars, attended gymnasium lessons when Mendelssohn was sixteen, corresponded with various intellectuals, and sought entrée into Berlin's scholarly circles. Gumpertz Inuuuunly though mostly in vain—sought teachers and patrons for himself, becoming close at one point to members of the Royal Academy of Science. His academic zenith was achieving the degree of medical doctor, but medical practice was of little interest to him. Despite his extensive knowledge, he published few of his writings, among them a slim volume in Hebrew—a commentary on Ibn Ezra's commentary on the five *Megilloth* to which he appended a general article on the value of science.

Gumpertz died young, and to Mendelssohn was left the fulfillment of the dreams of his mentor and close friend. Mendelssohn pursued his studies assiduously, improving his knowledge of languages—German, French, and English—in order to became better acquainted with the philosophical literature of his time. He later acknowledged that he never studied at a university, never listened to lectures at any academic college, achieving everything through diligence and his own efforts. With a satisfied retrospective glance, he pronounced himself a self-made man. From this standpoint Mendelssohn fulfilled the ideal of the Enlightenment: with his natural talents and intelligence a man can seize his own fate, escape the limitations into which he was born, and shape his own intellectual life.

Mendelssohn never wrote a detailed autobiographical account of his surprising transition from the "religious library" of Torah scholarship to the "library of arts and sciences" of scholars and philosophers. It emerges from his personal correspondence and theoretical writing, however, that by the end of the 1740s his inclination to study had become a passion to expand his intellectual circles, to read ever more science and philosophy, and to devote long hours to contemplation of philosophy. He had to close an enormous gap, cross the barrier of the European languages, adopt the lexicon of the Enlightenment and the grammar of contemporary culture, and become conversant with an entire multilayered world of European culture from classical Greece to Newton, Locke, Leibniz, and Rousseau. From his early youth, Mendelssohn wrote, he had devoted his leisure and rest to philosophy and the arts, to thoughts of his own vocation and the vocation of his Jewish brethren, to thinking as deeply as he could of human beings, of fate, and of divine providence. In his early manhood his inclination became clear toward philosophical study, toward the realm of reason and humanism, which in the eighteenth century was replacing theology as the most prestigious discipline. The first early-Enlightenment philosophical treatise he studied required a titanic effort. *An Essay Concerning Human Understanding*, by the English philosopher John Locke, existed at the time only in the original Latin. Using a dictionary Mendelssohn managed to read it and understand it, and he was influenced by Locke's pronouncements on the pleasures of philosophy. In the 1770s he was appalled when doctors ordered him to forgo excessive intellectual effort in order to safeguard his failing health. "Ah, philosophy!" he wrote in retrospect. "In my younger days you were my beloved wife who was my consolation in all my tribulations, and now . . . I shall fear to go to you as a man would fear approaching his beloved in whose bones resides decay. . . . And yet my desire for you heightened and I was unable to quell my desire, and would often risk my life to make love to you."

His use of erotic diction to describe his attraction to philosophy was not solely rhetorical; it expressed his worldview and his profoundest existential experience. In one of his first original essays, *Über die Empfindungen* (On sentiments), published anonymously in 1755, Mendelssohn set out what might be called a doctrine on pleasure in the aesthetics of philosophical study. Quite a few of the utterances of the protagonists in this essay's philosophical dialogue expressed the thrill of the young scholar at finding himself in an intellectual milieu of ideas. Philosophy, he proclaimed, is not only dry study of the world and its conventions, of principles and concepts, but also a fountainhead of pleasure. It might be thought that the young man from Dessau, a bachelor in his early twenties, who lived as an ascetic scholar, sacrificing himself for philosophical study, had substituted intellectual passion for sensual and erotic feelings. He chided those who characterized intellect as "disturbing our pleasure." Conversely, in the third letter of "On Sentiments" Mendelssohn presented a theory that included among its autobiographical elements a description of "how I prepare myself to enjoy something pleasurable":

> I contemplate the object of the pleasure, I reflect upon all sides of it, and strive to grasp them distinctly. Then I direct my attention to the general connection among them; I swing from the parts to the whole. . . . The contemplation of the structure of the world remains an inexhaustible source of pleasure for the philosopher. It sweetens his lonely hours, it fills his soul with the sublimest sentiments, withdrawing his thoughts from the dust of the earth and bringing them nearer to the throne of divinity. Because of his contemplations he must perhaps dispense with honor, sensual ecstasy, and riches; for him they are but dust upon which he treads with his feet.

The author derives pleasure from the basic philosophy of optimism that Mendelssohn learned from Leibniz: a sense of the entirety of experience, of the beauty and wonderful order of the universe, and of theodicy—the principle that this is the most perfect of all the possible worlds to be created by the Almighty. The philosopher undergoes a powerful emotional experience: "Then in bold flight swing over to the universal proportion of all these parts to the immeasurable whole. What heavenly rapture will suddenly surprise you! The study of philosophy, especially the aspiration to perfection, brings the philosopher to the brink of fainting: "In the numbing ecstasy you will scarcely be able to maintain your composure." This is a sublime pleasure dependent not upon humankind's basest weaknesses and drives "but on the rational striving for representations grounded in one another." Mathematics, too, which is generally perceived as lacking sparkle, becomes a source of sublime pleasure: "The amazing multiplicity of aspects embodies in the most pleasing order of all turns even mathematics into an occupation that heightens ecstasy." Therefore, Mendelssohn asserted, no happiness equals that of the philosopher: "No one who is acquainted with genuine reason and travels down its roads can doubt either the usefulness or the fullness of the pleasure that flows from its source." Philosophy's concern is man, his soul, consciousness of his existence, his aspiration to know God, and his predilection for perfection. "There lies in me an irresistible drive toward completeness and perfection," Mendelssohn wrote.

The intellectual transformation undergone by Mendelssohn in his teens and twenties was not a unique case. Israel Samoscz, Abraham Kisch, and Aaron Gumpertz were other young Jews of the eighteenth century whose talents and desires directed them toward the rabbinical elite but who were unable to find fulfillment there. In central and eastern Europe the early maskilim appeared: Jewish medical students from the universities of Padua in Italy and Frankfurt an der Oder and Halle in Prussia, physicians like Tuvia Cohen and Judah Leib Hurwitz, wandering Torah scholars like Baruch Shick of Shklov, scientists like Raphael Levy of Hanover, book printers, and religiously educated merchants, as well as several rabbis. The early Haskalah was not a consolidated movement, nor was it initiated or planned. It encompassed a broad spectrum of positions and styles—from a rabbi like Jacob Emden with a general interest in science to an ambitious scholar with a degree in medicine

like Aaron Gumpertz. It did, however, have common lines—
a sense of disquietude with cultural backwardness in the era
of significant development in Christian Europe, a tremendous
passion for secular knowledge; criticism of the limited range of
the religious library; aspiration to restore the neglected medieval philosophical heritage to that library; high regard for the
Hebrew language; and an increasing sense that the early maskilim, the "researchers" and "philosophers," who were subject
to the suspicion of the rabbinic elite, were becoming an intellectual elite in their own right.

When Mendelssohn found his vocation as a philosopher
in Berlin of the mid-eighteenth century in the company of
maskilim like Israel Samoscz and Aaron Gumpertz, he joined
the early Haskalah of European Jewry. An additional element,
however, made his career extraordinary. The early maskilim
built the renewed Jewish library while enriching it with books
in Hebrew on language, astronomy, mathematics, medicine,
and philosophy. In general terms they were active in the same
milieu as the traditional elite—the Hebrew printing presses,
the Jewish community of consumers and patrons, graduates
of traditional education who were members of the upper and
middle classes—but the early maskil Mendelssohn branched
out from that milieu into the world of German literature. This
extraordinary step inevitably drew attention.

Outside the homes of Berlin Jews, the German Enlightenment was revolutionizing the cultural and literary world. Pro-
fessors, government officials, clergymen, teachers, physicians,
jurists, and publishers joined forces as the Enlightenment intelligentsia to establish a Republic of Letters. In 1761 an eyewitness
wrote: "We are living in a century in which . . . almost all are
infected by the desire to be writers. From the palace to the
shepherd's hut, anyone who can hold a pen writes books." This
was the cultural climate that nourished Mendelssohn, and he
quickly reciprocated with his own contribution. Like other cul-

tured men in Germany, he recognized the difference between the moderate German Enlightenment and the radical Enlightenment of France, embodied by Voltaire, who questioned basic values of state and religion. Mendelssohn's identification with the German Enlightenment was absolute. In 1755, when Mendelssohn sent his literary protagonist of "On Sentiments"—the English philosopher Theocles (who speaks in Mendelssohn's voice)—to Germany, he had him stress the superiority of German Enlightenment over the "frivolous" French version, which was irresponsibly engaged in philosophizing and reasoning:

> The mixture of seductive imagination and French frivolity, peddled as metaphysics by so many of his countrymen, was so starkly at odds with his proclivity for rigor and fundamentals that he made the decision to renounce his fatherland, his tranquility, and his friends' embrace in order to search for a people that treasures accurate thinking more than free thinking. Germany seemed to him to hold out the promise of such a people. He read the immortal writings with which our countrymen have enriched the learned world in the past century, and people say that the soberness, indeed, the very dullness for which they are reproached by some petty critics, was one of the things that drove him to be acquainted with this nation.

Mendelssohn's unreserved support of the German Enlightenment—his predilection for "proper thinking" in an absolutist-supervised state over "free thinking"—was a cultural-patriotic declaration in this early work. In the decade since the young Mendelssohn had come from Dessau to seek a rabbinical career, he had traveled a long way along other roads. Now this Jewish philosopher from Berlin, this early maskil, was aspiring to become the ultimate spokesman of the leading trends in contemporary German culture.

3

Cultural Conversion: The Three Formative Years

IN THE early 1750s Mendelssohn joined the public sphere of the German Enlightenment. Through incessant study he gained a command of the fundamental essays of philosophical discourse, and he soon took his place among Berlin intellectuals. One of them, the writer and publisher Friedrich Nicolai, wrote in awe that when Mendelssohn discovered the philosophical world of Leibniz, Wolff, and Locke, and the theological concepts of rationalistic religion, "He suddenly found himself in a completely different world, for up to that time he had almost no idea about Christian theology or philosophy more recent than that of Maimonides."

Mendelssohn immediately connected with the rationalist philosophy of religion that had been common in Germany for several decades—natural theology which assumes that intellectual philosophical study is the way to know God and the fundamental truths of the world and humankind, to grasp, even without divine revelation, the Creation and the existence of an immortal soul. From the point of view of a believing Jew like Mendelssohn, this was an appropriate entry into a universal philosophical discourse that not only was unthreatening to religion but in fact reinforced its foundations. "Our common God," wrote Mendelssohn to a Christian friend, "is not the God of Jews or Christians, but the God of all human beings." As we have seen, one of the first philosophical works he read was Locke's *An Essay Concerning Human Understanding*, in which the author rejected the concept that man possesses innate principles and truths. Locke formulates a ramified system of concepts for understanding the processes of thought, cognition, and knowledge of truths through sensory experience and rational thinking. Mendelssohn eagerly accepted Locke's call to place theology on an intellectual footing, based on his essential premise regarding the tension existing in Enlightenment philosophy between the supernatural divine revelation described in the Scriptures and the supremacy of natural human intelligence. In the insights of Mendelssohn's philosophy of the Jewish religion, traces of Locke can be found: "When God illuminates [man's] soul with supernatural light [revelation], He does not extinguish his natural light"; sometimes, Mendelssohn continued, God reveals truths to man through natural intelligence, sometimes through miracles. Revelation is no more than the expansion of the natural light, and religion does not run counter to reason. Mendelssohn viewed Leibniz as the greatest philosopher, always adhering to his optimistic principles: that perfect harmony exists in the world, that ours is the best of all possible worlds created by the Almighty, and justification always exists for apparent evil and injustice. This, for Mendelssohn, was "the true philosophy," as opposed to the sham "French" version that undermined social and religious order.

In early 1753 Aaron Gumpertz took Mendelssohn to one of Berlin's scholars' clubs and introduced him to Gotthold

Ephraim Lessing, the son of a Lutheran clergyman. Lessing, who was Mendelssohn's age and lived not far from him in the center of Berlin, was one of the most prominent men in German Enlightenment circles. The two played chess and from their first meeting found a common language that became the foundation of a long and celebrated friendship; that friendship was to be one of the sources of Mendelssohn's social standing and his entrée into Enlightenment social circles. Lessing became his most fervent admirer. "Mendelssohn," he wrote a short time after they became friends, "really is a Jew, a man of twenty and some years who without any guidance has achieved a great strength in languages, in mathematics, in philosophy, in poetry. I regard him as a future honor to his nation."

The years 1753 to 1755 were the most important and critical in the shaping of the young Moses Mendelssohn. During those years, from age twenty-four to twenty-six, he finally broke away from his training as a Torah scholar destined to take his place in the religious elite, and instead joined the scholarly elite of Berlin. Lessing, Nicolai, and others became his friends, he published his first philosophical essays in German, and he initiated the first of a series of Jewish Enlightenment projects — the weekly journal *Kohelet Musar* (Preacher of morals). At the same time he climbed several rungs up the social ladder, and began a personal and business association with Isaac Bernhard, who owned a silk factory. In 1750 Bernhard hired Mendelssohn as his children's tutor and took him into his house. Mendelssohn was much admired by the Bernhard family. He went to work in the factory as a bookkeeper and eventually became a partner, with an annual salary of three hundred thalers. His financial situation gradually improved, freeing him for literary pursuits. In the silk factory office Mendelssohn found time to read, write short essays, and receive visiting colleagues; between times he kept the factory's books.

Beginning in the 1750s, however, Jews in Berlin fell under

the shadow of constant threat from the Prussian state. King Friedrich II, who was renowned throughout Europe for political and military wisdom, had turned Prussia into a continental power. He also was known as an enlightened monarch who fostered culture. But in 1750 Friedrich decided to tighten supervision over the Jews. He sent a message steeped in suspicion to the Berlin Jewish community. Jews were inferior, he declared, and were "tolerated" (*geduldet*) only by grace of the royal house. A rigid policy devoid of Enlightenment values—or indeed human ones—determined the fate of the Jews for years to come. The draconic edict, *Revidierte General Privilegium und Reglement*, began:

> We, Friedrich, by the grace of God, King of Prussia . . . make known and order to make known: We have noticed in our kingdom of Prussia . . . and particularly in this capital, various faults and abuses among the licensed and tolerated Jews, and have particularly observed that the rampant increase of these abuses has caused enormous damage and hardship, not only to the public, particularly to the Christian inhabitants and merchants. . . . For this reason we have found it necessary to make such provision that this, our most gracious purpose, may be attained, so that a proportion may be maintained between Christian and Jewish business opportunities and trades, and that neither [Jew or Christian] may be injured through a prohibited expansion of Jewish business activity.

Jews were divided into six groups according to their economic benefit to the state. Only a small group of the wealthy elite were accorded the desirable "general privilege": in exchange for payment they received freedom of residence and movement, as well as trading rights equal to those of the Christian merchants. The next rank consisted of less prosperous Jews; a member of this class received some protection but was restricted to a specific place of residence and could transfer his limited privilege only to a single son. A third group, including such vital professionals as physicians, spectacle makers, and minters, was defined as "specially protected Jews," with no right of inheritance. Among the lower-order groups were community employees— rabbis, religious judges, cantors, synagogue treasurers, gravediggers, and the "tolerated"— people who lived under the aegis of the upper class and who had no rights but were granted permission for temporary residence in the city. Private tutors like Mendelssohn were lumped together with servants in the least privileged order. People in this category were expressly forbidden to marry within the city limits under penalty of expulsion. A list appended to the *Reglement* determined who would be permitted to live in Berlin. The policy was clear: the impoverished, tramps, peddlers, and anyone not contributing to production and trade was barred from the city. The number of Jews would not increase, and Jewish gatekeepers would guarantee this, as stipulated in Clause 12:

> It has already been decreed many times that Jewish beggars are nowhere to be allowed to cross our borders. . . . In the event that any such Jewish beggars nevertheless reach our capital surreptitiously, they shall be brought at once to the Poor Jews Home at the Prenzlau Gate. There they are to be given alms and on the following day evicted through the gate without being allowed to enter into the city.

Except for the small group that contributed to the mercantile state, whose economy was based on ensuring a positive trade balance, the Jews were defined as the undesirable, unpopular, suspect, immoral "other" on the margins of society. Comte Honoré Mirabeau, one of the Enlightenment's liberal spokesmen and later a leader of the French Revolution, dubbed Friedrich's edict as "a law worthy of cannibals."

It was against this backdrop that Mendelssohn—the alien private tutor from Dessau, a servant of the wealthy elite, the "tolerated" Jew, as he was legally defined by the Prussian state—joined the assembly of savants. His meetings with Lessing and others took place in "the Learned Coffeehouse," where every week an exclusive group of mathematicians, physicists, physicians, officials, and theologians would meet for evenings of readings, discussion, debate, chess, and billiards. They occasionally met at the Monday Club, which was even more exclusive and among whose denizens were members of the Royal Academy of Science, artists, musicians, and philosophers. From the perspective of the absolutist state—in Prussia and elsewhere—such gatherings were subversive, venues for unrestricted, unsupervised discourse, far from the eyes of the king and his officials, and far from the ecclesiastical establishment. Even in England, there were attempts in the first half of the century to close down clubs suspected of subversive discourse. The enlightened Prussians were mostly conservative, supporters of the monarchy and even of religion, and it would be erroneous to view their clubs and coffeehouses as subversive groups whose members sought to undermine state order. Nevertheless, gatherings of the enlightened intelligentsia created a new framework for the dissemination of public opinion, which in turn embodied possibilities of crossing the borders stipulated by the government's laws and bureaucratic procedures. And indeed, King Friedrich, whose police apparatus kept him informed about almost everything happening in his kingdom, knew full well about the fame and prestige of Mendelssohn but declined to meet with him or add royal approval to his respected status in the scholarly community. Thus the friendship and intellectual respect of Lessing and other Gentile scholars for the Jewish Gumpertz and Mendelssohn carried particular weight.

Gumpertz had been part of these circles for some years. Beginning in the mid-1740s he was secretary to Jean-Baptiste de Boyer, Marquis d'Argens, who was *Kammerherr,* director of the Prussian Royal Academy of Science. After completing his medical studies he served another director of the Academy, Pierre-Louis de Maupertuis, and thus established connections with learned circles through which he assisted in Mendelssohn's entrée. Both men broke into the Enlightenment Republic of Letters, and Mendelssohn in particular achieved immediate acclaim. His first philosophical essay, *Über die Wahrscheinlichkeit* (Thoughts on probability), was given an anonymous public reading at the Learned Coffeehouse before members of the Society of Friends of Literature. When the reader committed a verbal error, Mendelssohn immediately corrected him, thus revealing his authorship, amazing the audience, and cementing his place in the intellectual elite. The ascent of the Jewish wunderkind from an alien cultural background became a Cinderella story in these circles. He is a true Jew, it was said of him, still very young but a genius who, uninstructed, had become accomplished in all the sciences. Apart from the club and coffeehouse meetings, Mendelssohn was also occasionally invited to some of the scholars' homes, introducing him to a lifelong social niche. Mendelssohn's emergence into the public milieu was promoted by Lessing, who commended him warmly to his intellectual colleagues. "I render thanks to Providence," Mendelssohn wrote some thirty years after meeting Lessing, "for the blessing it conferred upon me by introducing me so early in life . . . to a man who formed my soul and was always at my side as a judge of the good and beautiful." Lessing took a keen interest in Mendelssohn's career as a philosopher, encouraging him in original writing and taking upon himself the responsibility of having his first essays printed in the 1750s.

In 1749 his friendship with Gumpertz inspired Lessing to write *Die Juden,* a play that was not printed until five years later. It was a light comedy, but its protagonist was a high-minded, cultured, and magnanimous man, and the revelation of this character as a Jew forces the reader to confront the stereotypes current in Christian culture—the mendacious Jew, morally inferior, and culturally backward—and the concomitant legal and social barriers that had existed for generations between Jews and Christians. Lessing and other eighteenth-century playwrights considered drama a substitute for preaching, a medium for moral education. "The theater should be a school of the moral world," said Lessing. His play's Jewish protagonist, based on Gumpertz, was meant to present an image of the new Jew, and to assert the possibility that a Jew could be an exemplary, educated, moral citizen.

In the summer of 1754 the *Göttingische Anzeigen von gelehrten Sachen* published a critique of *Die Juden* by Johann David Michaelis, a Göttingen University professor. Michaelis's claim was simple and trenchant: a good dramatist is committed to putting real-life characters onstage. Enjoyment of the drama is impaired when he chooses a preposterous character who everyone knows does not exist in life. Jews, Michaelis wrote, were hostile toward Christianity by the very nature of their religion, and immoral by virtue of their traditional occupation with trade, which compels them almost by definition to deceive their customers. Given these realities, he concluded, it was hard to imagine that a Jew could assume the exemplary character of Lessing's fictional protagonist.

Mendelssohn was already keeping track of German Enlightenment literature, and Michaelis's article both angered and humiliated him—and inspired a crucial reaction. So long as cultural barriers restricted Jews to their own internal religious discourse, conducted mostly in the court of the rabbinic elite, they had scant opportunity to respond to hostile displays. Suspicion of Jews was perceived as normal by attackers and victims alike. But once a Jewish intellectual was accepted into the group of scholars and took part in their discourse, public confrontation of such prejudice, employing the lexicon of the Enlightenment, became both possible and necessary. This was a challenge that only a Jew who had moved from the periphery into the center of the literary and ideological world could take up.

A few days after reading Michaelis's critique, Mendelssohn composed a rebuttal in the form of an anonymous letter to Gumpertz, the model for the protagonist of *Die Juden*. Lessing published the letter in the journal he edited, *Die Theatralische Bibliotek* (The theatrical library). Armed with the terminology, values, and worldviews of the Enlightenment, and having been accepted as a full member in that milieu, Mendelssohn published his first article attacking religious intolerance.

This was his first Enlightenment test—and a test of the Enlightenment itself for those prejudiced against Jews. Mendelssohn cast himself as the intellectual invoking, according to the supreme values of humanism and reason, the principle of religious tolerance toward his coreligionists. In rebutting Michaelis, Mendelssohn adopted a tone of self-assurance but also revealed a powerful sense of humiliation. Reading it gives us a first look under the skin of this man of twenty-five years as he realizes to his consternation that the reception he had been given by Lessing and his friends in Berlin was still far from common. Painfully, Mendelssohn wrote:

> These thoughts made me blush with shame. . . . What a humiliation for our oppressed nation! What exaggerated contempt! That ordinary Christian people have from time immemorial regarded us as the dregs of nature, as open sores on human society. But from learned people I have always expected a juster judgment. . . . Is it not enough that we must feel the bitterest hatred of the Christians in so many cruel ways; are these injustices against us to be justified by calumnies?

Jews are prepared, Mendelssohn wrote, in a daring critique of the restrictive policies of Friedrich II, to continue being oppressed; in the midst of free and happy citizens Jews live under continual restrictions. They could accept this bitter fate and even bear the contempt and mockery of the whole world, but they must demand acknowledgment of their capacity for only virtue, the sole comfort of oppressed souls, the sole refuge of the abandoned. For a scholar to deny even the possibility that Jews might be enlightened, learned, and moral is, Mendelssohn declared, a position contrary to reason and humanity. In this civil and legal congeries of oppression and discrimination, he demanded, Jews must be left at least the possibility of cultivating themselves as individuals.

In these sentiments one cannot but hear the hurt Mendelssohn speaking on his own behalf as well as Gumpertz's. True, his concept of the Enlightenment was far from radical. He was not about to take the revolutionary step of criticizing Prussian government policy; he was resigned to the status of the Jews as defined by the 1750 legislation. But he claimed at least the right for a Jew to develop as an individual, and even to be acknowledged as a man both learned and virtuous. Michaelis, in his implied critique of Mendelssohn and Gumpertz as learned and enlightened Jews, denied such a possibility.

Mendelssohn was confronted with an early existential question. In his play, Mendelssohn wrote, Lessing sought to arouse public opinion and through the character of the Jew to convey his truth: that the image of the Jews must change. Mendelssohn inquired whether the reviewer was merely a theologian expressing a Christian position whereby all Jews are despicable murderers and robbers. "I would not wish to think of Christianity," he wrote naïvely, "as being founded on rejection of all humanistic values." And in any case, he added, anyone familiar with the Jews knows that few are criminals and almost none are murderers; most Jews, he wrote, are industrious, moderate, charitable people who maintain the sanctity of marriage and are exemplary citizens. Some are eminent learned men like Gumpertz who could in fact fill the role of Lessing's protagonist. Audiences, Mendelssohn concluded, might undergo a corrective emotional experience—they would be shocked by the extremes of anti-Jewish hatred, then accept that Jews, too, are human beings.

After 1754, when Mendelssohn first became aware of the conflict in enlightened public opinion between prejudice and religious tolerance, he realized that his vocation lay not only in the philosophical study he craved but also in the struggle to universalize that simple conclusion, deriving from reason, natural rights, and humanism: that a Jew is a human being.

Michaelis, as far as Mendelssohn was concerned, had failed miserably the test of the Enlightenment. But only a year later Michaelis published a warm review of Mendelssohn's first two books. Without revealing the author's identity, Michaelis shared with the readers of the *Göttingische Anzeigen* his excitement at the entry of a Jew into the learned community:

> We cannot conceal from our readers the fact that in all matters pertaining to [the author's] way of life he is not part of the world of learning, and he should not be sought among the members of the Christian faith but among the Jews. This only serves to heighten our enjoyment of his book since thus far our attention was only given to its subject and style, without our knowing from what kind of unpredictable author this perfect book has come.

Michaelis addressed the two philosophical essays written by the young Mendelssohn and published anonymously by Lessing in Berlin in 1755, *Philosophischen Gespräche* (Philosophical dialogues) and *Über die Empfindungen* (On sentiments). At the center of the first essay, modeled on Socratic dialogue, were Leibniz's key optimistic ideas—of preestablished harmony and of theodicy. Mendelssohn elucidated his basic philosophical premises, interspersed them with criticism of Leibniz's proofs, and introduced Baruch Spinoza into the discussion. In the first pages of the first philosophical text published by Mendelssohn, his admiration for Spinoza, the Jewish philosopher from Amsterdam who predated him by a century, is evident. In the first dialogue Mendelssohn sought to prove that Leibniz had borrowed the idea of preestablished harmony from Spinoza and had only concealed this fact for tactical purposes; in the second dialogue Mendelssohn sought to acquit Spinoza of the charge of atheism.

Admiration of Spinoza in the eighteenth century was problematic since he had been accused of instigating a master plot against religious faiths; the name Spinoza had become synonymous with heresy. In the view of the historian Jonathan Israel, for instance, Spinoza's philosophy, especially his criticism of religion and his pantheism—in shorthand *Deus sive Natura*, God or Nature—nourished the radical European Enlightenment and agitated the intellectual milieu for decades. Even Mendelssohn, who throughout his life resisted atheistic notions, admitted that Spinoza's pantheism was finally a tragic mistake and sought to divorce his sentiments about religion from his exemplary philosophy. Mendelssohn displayed an inner tension between admiration and rejection:

> Before the transition from the Cartesian to the Leibnizian philosophy could occur, it was necessary for someone to take the plunge into the monstrous abyss lying between them. This unhappy lot fell to Spinoza. How his fate is to be pitied! He was a sacrifice for the human intellect, but one that deserves to be decorated with flowers. Without him, philosophy would never have been able to extend its borders so far.

Mendelssohn may have identified with Spinoza as a daring Jewish philosopher, and may also have taken as a cautionary tale the

heavy price paid by Spinoza in 1656 when he was excommunicated by the Jewish community. As one of the interlocutors says
in Mendelssohn's "Philosophical Dialogues":

> The misfortune of this man has always touched me in an
> extraordinary way. He lived in moderation, alone and irre
> proachable; he renounced all human idols and devoted his
> entire life to reflection, and look what happened! In the laby
> rinth of his meditations, he goes astray, and, out of error,
> maintains much that agrees very little with his innocent way
> of life, and that the most depraved scoundrel might wish for
> in order to be able to indulge his evil desires with impunity.
> How unjust is the irreconcilable hatred of scholars toward
> someone so unfortunate!

This awareness of Spinoza's fate plagued Mendelssohn throughout his life, and he diligently followed the paths trodden by
philosophers for whom reason and religious faith were integral parts of their doctrine. Thus, for instance, Mendelssohn
often dissociated himself from the works of Voltaire, Europe's
enfant terrible. For him Voltaire represented the radical, frivolous philosophy that typified the French Enlightenment. In the
second edition of "Philosophical Dialogues" Mendelssohn took
Leibniz's part against Voltaire's satirical critique in one of the
masterworks of the Enlightenment, *Candide*. The fictional adventure story of the naïve Candide, published in 1759, is a trenchant assessment of the terrible injustices wrought by the religious establishment, hardhearted rulers, lecherous priests, the
Inquisition, warped values, and cynical politics. At the same
time it indicts optimistic philosophers like the ludicrous Doctor Pangloss, who despite all his travails continues to spout
Leibniz's optimistic slogans—what is happening is what had
to happen, for "all is for the best in this best of all possible
worlds." Mendelssohn contended that not only was this criticism unfair and the descriptions of the horrors perpetrated by

human beings against one another exaggerated, but Voltaire had evaded serious engagement with Leibniz's optimistic philosophy and had failed to refute the basic premise that a more perfect world was impossible. Mendelssohn admired Spinoza and was amused by Voltaire's satire, but from his first appearance he positioned himself as a moderate Enlightenment philosopher, believing in God as the absolute good and in the possibility of humankind's happiness, and far from the radical pole occupied by critics of religion, society, and state.

An optimistic philosophy also emerges from "On Sentiments": man can attain happiness because the world provides everything he needs to attain a sense of perfection, which is the most sublime spiritual and sensual pleasure he can experience. "Everything in nature aspires to a single purpose," says one interlocutor in this epistolary dialogue, articulating Leibniz's idea that "everything is founded on everything, everything is— perfect." But for Mendelssohn matters were not that simple. He placed the concept of beauty and the feeling of pleasure on different levels and acknowledged that some sensual pleasure is fleeting and inferior to the refined pleasure of the philosopher. According to Mendelssohn, anyone swept away by his lusts will be deaf to reason. Sublime pleasure could be attained only by those subscribing to Maimonides' ideal: scholars and thinkers, men of reason seeking perfection, engaged in constant observation and deliberation and capable of approaching the knowledge of God.

In the last part of "On Sentiments" Mendelssohn expresses his views on the eighteenth-century debate about the legitimacy of suicide. Is man master of his own life? How can an atheist be persuaded not to take his own life? Is there any situation in which death is preferable to life? In a series of rational arguments Mendelssohn rejected suicide, claiming that it runs counter to reason and man's vocation of striving for perfection. In any case, he wrote, death is not a condition of annihilation or a return to a primal state of deep sleep, for God would not allow his children to remain in such a state, unperfected, for eternity. Thus even the deist, who does not believe in either the divine revelation of Christianity or Judaism, cannot justify suicide: "Whoever, on the basis of the light of reason, assumes a future life must allow for a connection between the future life and the present one. . . . Whoever does not wait for the end of the duration allotted to him in this world plunges himself into a future state completely different from the state into which he would have been transported by the course of nature."

The last part of "On Sentiments" reads like a humanistic sermon. On the one hand Mendelssohn addresses the premise that human beings can take pleasure in acts of cruelty, and on the other he attempts to explain the operation of compassion in the face of human suffering. He vehemently repudiates atrocities perpetrated by human beings: blood sports such as jousting or the cockfights popular in England. "In the case of some bloody amusements," Mendelssohn wrote, "one must, so to say, suppress all sympathy, all human feeling, if one wants to find them gratifying." It may have been the Romans' disregard for their slaves' lives, for instance, that inured them to the dreadful sight of gladiators in combat with wild animals. This philosophical essay ends with a shocking critical description of a public execution, a ritual that drew the masses to eighteenth-century European city squares. Mendelssohn, who apparently witnessed one such execution, expresses his horror:

> Look at the crowd that in thick heaps swarms around someone condemned to die. They have all understood what things the scoundrel has perpetrated; they abhor his conduct and maybe even the man himself. Now he is dragged, disfigured and powerless, to the gruesome scaffold. People work their way through the throng, they stand on their tiptoes, they climb on roofs in order to see the features of death distort his face. His judgment is pronounced; the executioner ap-

proaches him; in an instant his fate will be decided. How longingly at this moment do all hearts wish that he were forgiven! This man? The object of their revulsion whom a moment ago they would themselves have condemned to death? By what means now does a ray of human love become alive in them once again? Is it not the approach of the punishment, the sight of the most gruesome physical evil, which somehow reconciles us even with someone wicked and purchases for him our love? Without love we could not possibly be sympathetic toward his fate.

Mendelssohn did not subscribe to the fashionable pessimistic idea that death was preferable to a life of suffering. His first two essays published in 1755 resonated with the love of man and a belief in man's ability to approach perfection. He affirmed life, recoiled from cruelty, and vilified suicide; he insisted on the possibility of happiness, perfection, enjoyment, and pleasure in this world and sought to prove the immortality of the soul. In the course of his transition from rabbinic culture to that of the European Enlightenment, he identified the deepest fears of mid-eighteenth-century man as the educated elites' enchanted world of religion began to fade. As skeptical, critical thinking challenged religious truths based on divine revelation or on assurances of religious establishments, modern man needed new anchors by which he could moor himself so as not to be swept into atheistic despair or morally unbridled hedonism. Mendelssohn, who had apparently experienced similar uncertainty during his formative years, when his religious worldview was coalescing, focused as a philosopher on placating these fears. In his view, living without God and submitting to base instincts were the greatest of all evils. He wrote in "On Sentiments": "The human being who arms himself with the weapons of reason against this seductress [of contemptible sensual pleasures] acts wisely and trusts her only when no future contradicts her." The secret of his success as a philosopher lies in providing insight to anyone seeking to maintain faith in God, in the triumph of life over death, in the uniqueness of man and his immortal soul, in man's virtues, and in his ability to experience sensual and spiritual pleasure in the context of a modest, serene family life.

Later that productive year some of these ideas were translated into a remarkable Hebrew text. In Berlin in 1755, Mendelssohn and his friend Tobias Bock published the first issue of the weekly *Kohelet Musar*. At first glance this seems an immature and feeble attempt to found a first journal for a Jewish readership. The weekly was short-lived—only two issues (of eight pages each) were published. *Kohelet Musar* apparently left little impression at the time, and today only a few copies have survived. It was printed without a date or the name of the printing house, without the names of its writers; it had no eye-catching front page, and its circulation was negligible. But deeper scrutiny shows it to have been a text of revolutionary significance for Jewish culture. For the first time maskilim attempted to introduce an innovative medium into their culture by adopting the model popular and influential in England, Germany, and other countries of disseminating ideas through a "moral weekly." For the first time, some of the moderate Enlightenment's ideas were conveyed to the Jewish reader by means of the Hebrew language familiar to the learned elite and associated with the world of its scholars. Most significant, the publication of a journal devoted to moral reformation constituted a subversive step against the absolute authority of the religious elite over moral and cultural discourse. In a culture where public guidance, religious supervision, and the public voice had been the exclusive purview of rabbis, preachers, religious scholars, or Kabbalists, the two young writers from Berlin sought to make an alternative voice heard, the voice of the maskilim, the intellectuals not numbered among the rabbinic elite.

Although Mendelssohn and his friend employed maxims

from the Talmud and quotations from the treatises of Maimonides, Judah Halevi, and other Jewish thinkers to demonstrate that they were not imitating the outside culture but merely offering a new reading of Jewish religious thought, they in fact intended for *Kohelet Musar* to disseminate modern values unfamiliar to Ashkenazi society of the time. In the weekly's first article Mendelssohn surprised his Jewish readers by providing them with a formula for a worthy and happy life. The text's culturally rich, high-register Hebrew limited the potential readership to men from the religious elite. In their traditional religious value system, Torah study and observance of the religious precepts were the foundations of an ideal life; now a window was opened for them in the walls of the study hall, allowing them a new perspective on man as man, nature, the pleasures of life, aesthetics, and God. Man is the lord of Creation, Mendelssohn wrote, and by God's grace he can enjoy the goodness and beauty of a harmonious, breathtaking, perfect world—the best of all possible worlds. Go out into nature, he exhorted his reader, look at its flora and fauna, breathe, smell the spring blossom and relish it. The path to God, he declared, does not pass solely through the sacred texts but is blazed by veneration of the perfection of Creation.

"And you, Man!" wrote Mendelssohn with all the pathos of the ancient Hebrew prophets, "God labors for you, because of you valleys will be adorned with grass and beneath your feet flowers and herbage will burgeon, look and see the plain all around welcoming you as a beloved wife, a beauteous woman who paints her eyes with henna and comes wearing precious jewels to the love of her life." This text, which opens *Kohelet Musar*, reads like the young Mendelssohn's Rite of Spring— flowing, illuminating, joyful, and filled with promise. Against the backdrop of prevalent Hebrew and Yiddish books of ethics of Mendelssohn's generation—which depicted a world of gloomy hues and enjoined strict caution, even terror and fear of the punishments a sinner can expect—the Berlin weekly promised a new and better life.

The next article to appear in *Kohelet Musar* took up the battle of the Hebrew language that had been left abandoned by generations of scholars who concentrated solely on the Talmudic text. The article called for a revival of Hebrew, renewed Bible study, and out of this perfect language the creation of a literature all but unknown in recent Ashkenazi culture. Mendelssohn brought Leibniz's optimistic doctrine to his Hebrew readers. He dramatically described all the tribulations of life— man's dread of disease, crime, rulers' harsh edicts, war, imprisonment, slavery, loss of property, fraud, and of course, death— all in order to pacify the fearful reader and assure him that all God's works are for the best and beyond reproach. Evil in the world has an acceptable explanation, though man may be incapable of understanding how seeming evil may be, from God's point of view, good.

The subversiveness of this moral weekly lay not in denigration of religion; quite the opposite. In his own way Mendelssohn strove to embrace the truths of religion and even stressed the duty of observance of the religious precepts through philosophical insights on Man's vocation and the nature of the world and of God. He declared, for example, "And know that the love of God is the joy of knowing His perfection, and from this will come the desire to hear His voice and observe His commandments." He did not, however, employ the traditional rhetorical means of the preacher; he declined to instil fear of punishment or to demand obedience of the Torah and the rabbis. Rather, he was a new kind of moralist, a philosophical guide. In the second issue he leveled keen social criticism that revealed his budding sensitivity toward matters of social justice. He excoriated the corrupt wealthy elite and hypocritical, sanctimonious clerics who misled innocent believers, while at the same time adjuring his readers to take pity on the poor, starving thief or the dispossessed man. He concluded his homily with a description of the schema of the ideal man, the decent bourgeois who divides his day efficaciously and sets a good example. Benjamin Franklin, scientist, inventor, philosopher, and ideologue of the American Revolution defined the ideal Enlightenment man of culture by emphasizing order, a rational division of time, and meticulous self-examination. Such a man would begin the morning by asking himself what good he might do today, and end the evening with an accounting of what good he had done. For Mendelssohn the day of *Yeda'aya Ish-Emuna* (a man of faith and erudition) begins in the early morning with study and prayer, continues with the negotiations, business, and commerce he conducts with blamelessness and modesty, and ends in the bosom of his patriarchal family, at whose head he stands and whom he educates: "And in the evening he will return to his home and rest from his labors, surrounded by his children as olive saplings; they will be happy at his return and he will be happy to see them, his wife will attend him, and he will instruct them in righteousness and in the way of knowledge will he teach them and adjure them to justice and charity."

In *Kohelet Musar* Mendelssohn turned the intellectual writer into one of the spokesmen in the Jewish public sphere. He hoped to create something that existed in the European Enlightenment but not yet in the Jewish world—the public opinion of a readership that might expand in numbers and influence to become a decisive factor in society. As we have seen, this first enterprise of Mendelssohn's left little impression on Jewish society—at least in part because its readers, made up entirely of members of the religious elite, recognized its subversive aims and identified its inherent threat. One of Mendelssohn's first biographers wrote that the rabbis "created such a great outcry that the modest savant retreated and publication of the journal was ceased." Many years later, at the end of Mendelssohn's life, a more successful journal made its appearance: *Hame'asef*, the principal organ of the Jewish Enlightenment movement when it reached its zenith in central Europe in the 1780s. But pride of place in the history of Jewish journals belongs to Mendelssohn's *Kohelet Musar*.

4

War and Peace, Love and Family,
Fame and Frustration

FROM AUTUMN 1756 to winter 1763 the Seven Years' War raged on various battlefields throughout central Europe, involving all the major European powers and exacting a toll of close to one million lives. The war had begun with a successful preemptive strike by Prussia against the perceived ambition of Austria, France, and Russia to undermine the German state. But it became a war of survival for Friedrich II. Tens of thousands of troops were killed, the economy's resources dwindled, and in 1760 Berlin even fell briefly into the hands of Russian troops. Prussia was perceived as an aggressor, supported only by England, France's rival for control over colonies in America, Africa, and Asia. At the height of the war Voltaire wrote *Candide;* in its first pages the voice of the critical philosopher is heard rousing public opinion against the "heroic butchery" taking place on European soil. He trenchantly criticized the hopelessness of a war whose aims were unclear and whose effect was calamitous human suffering. No one who had walked on a battlefield among the wretched, bleeding casualties, no one who had witnessed severed limbs or razed villages or raped women could believe that this was the best of all possible worlds. Voltaire leveled bitter satirical criticism at Prussian militarism and at an undeservedly celebrated king of Prussia.

Moses Mendelssohn, too, anxiously followed the unfolding events of the war and the successes and failures of the Prussian army. He served as a patriotic spokesman on behalf of the Berlin Jewish community, writing and translating into German sermons and poems in praise of king and country. To mark Prussian victories Jews held thanksgiving ceremonies in the synagogue, anthems were composed in Hebrew and German, and special sermons were delivered by the community rabbi, which were then forwarded to the royal court as an expression of loyalty and support. Military pressure so increased on Prussia that collapse seemed imminent, but a turnabout in the middle of 1762 saved Friedrich II's kingdom: the czarina of Russia died suddenly, and her successor signed a peace treaty with Prussia. A few months later, in February 1763, the Peace of Hubertusburg ended the Seven Years' War with Prussia territorially intact, a victorious European power.

On Saturday, March 12, 1763, at a special ceremony for the Berlin Jewish community at the synagogue, Rabbi Aaron Mosessohn (successor to Rabbi David Fränkel, who had died during the war) delivered the "Peace Sermon" written by Mendelssohn, who later translated it into German. Mendelssohn's sermon—which another author might have rendered nothing more than a series of phrases flattering the king, an expression of solidarity of Jews with the destiny of the country that graciously allowed them a place within its borders, and a declaration of fealty to Friedrich—became an Enlightenment text. The "Peace Sermon" became a humanistic protest against war and needless bloodshed. The sermon offers thanks not for military triumph, for "our hand raised against God's groaning and suffering creatures," but for renewal of the ethos of humanistic behavior; neither is it a forum for Schadenfreude against the vanquished, for "our joy is no longer over another's loss." Mendelssohn, of course, could not set himself up, like the subversive Voltaire, as an outspoken critic of the foolish policies of European crowned heads, but he described the terrible destruction and atrocities of war unstintingly:

> During the War our granaries were empty, diligence was to no avail. . . . At a time of war Man has no recompense, the cities are burned, the palaces destroyed, and all the magnificent edifices of learning and charity are shattered, religions are trampled underfoot, masterworks are looted, and all that our ancestors invented over several centuries for the benefit of humankind is destroyed in short order.

Peace, on the other hand, "is the essence of The Creation! Peace is the amity of living creatures! Peace is true happiness in Heaven!" Only God in his mercy. according to the rabbi's delivery of Mendelssohn's text, had saved Europe from the horrors of the war. War contradicts God's beneficial influence on all His creatures. God expects people to love one another: "Remember that we are the children of One God, we all have one Father, and One God created us to honor him and engraved in our heart the religion of nature and love of our fellow men." By internalizing humanistic values men could ensure peace and eschew war, the greatest enemy of divine and human order: "We have tasted and seen the evil and badness of making war on our neighbors. . . . We have learned to discern that it is not beasts of prey that make the land barren when there is hostility, hatred, envy and contention . . . strife and war, devastation and chaos." Mendelssohn's patriotic spokesmanship during the Seven Years' War elevated his status in the Berlin Jewish community. In April 1763, a few weeks after the thanksgiving ceremony marking the end of the war, the leaders of the community met to extend a special token of esteem to Mendelssohn, exempting him from community taxes: "For Moses this will be a special right over and above those enjoyed by the members of our community, free of all levies and taxes, for as long as he resides in our community." Exemption from taxes was usually enjoyed only by community rabbis and great religious scholars, and extension of this privilege to a scholar like Mendelssohn was extraordinary. This recognition of the Jewish philosopher took into account the advantages of his fame: Mendelssohn's public status had become an asset the community could exploit to strengthen the links between the Jews of Berlin and the larger community.

The famous Mendelssohn was of particular importance in building the group that was signatory to this decision—the heads of the elite families of merchants and wealthy businessmen, the most prominent of whom were the families of Veitel Heine Ephraim and Daniel Itzig. During the Seven Years' War the two families amassed vast fortunes as Masters of the Royal Mint. In order to cope with huge expenditures and prevent economic collapse, they debased Prussian coins by reducing their weight and alloying inexpensive metals to the coins' silver and gold. At the end of the war the return obtained by the "Mint Jews" made them extremely wealthy men and their economic power helped them secure government privileges and critical influence, shared with their families and business partners, within the Berlin Jewish community. From the 1760s to the end of the century the Ephraims and Itzigs were the leaders of Berlin Jewry. The rise of a wealthy Jewish elite, which spread to banking and the textile industry as well, encouraged a trend toward integration. The elite adopted the European lifestyle of the time. They maintained close ties with the bureaucrats who administered the economy of the absolutist state, identifying with its aims and even with its fundamental ethos—economic industriousness generating benefits for the state. They ascribed unprecedented importance to the image of Jews in the eyes of both public opinion and the government and its officials. Accordingly, the Ephraim and Itzig families fostered Mendelssohn's standing in the Jewish community, financially supported some of his literary enterprises and those of other young intellectuals, and viewed him as a kind of uncrowned leader who represented the Jews with dignity in the general economic and public milieu.

As the elite recognized the double-edged attitudes toward Jews—on the one hand, residual suspicion on the part of King Friedrich, who had signed the draconian edict of 1750, on the other, encouragement of the ethos of moral and industrious citizenship—Mendelssohn's status became a tool for advancement of Jewish interests and reduction of the restrictions against them. Mendelssohn's emergence during the war years as an esteemed philosopher and an increasingly prominent member of Enlightenment intelligentsia made him an attractive candidate to the affluent Jewish community for the role of the Berlin Jewish community's representative Jew.

Lessing left Berlin in 1756 but sustained his friendship with Mendelssohn through letters; meanwhile, Mendelssohn's social circle continued to widen. He spent a great deal of time, for instance, with the publisher Friedrich Nicolai, who at the time lived in the house that Mendelssohn and his family were to occupy from 1762. "I visit Nicolai in his garden quite frequently," he wrote to Lessing. "We read poetry, Nicolai shows me his work, and I sit in judgment as critic and admirer, laughing and censoring until nightfall." The muses did not fall silent during the Seven Years' War, and Mendelssohn was extraordinarily prolific. He published dozens of articles in literary and philosophical journals published by his German Enlightenment friends, wrote numerous book reviews and several philosophical essays, and translated various works into German, the most important of which was Jean-Jacques Rousseau's ground-breaking but controversial *Discourse on the Origin and Basis of Inequality Among Men*. Like many philosophers of his time, Mendelssohn rejected Rousseau's pessimistic perspective, according to which civilization was destroying the attributes of natural, free, and happy man, but his translation of this masterwork of Enlightenment culture was an achievement in itself. In 1759 he began studying Greek with the rector of the gymnasium and succeeded in translating several parts of Plato's *The Republic*. Between 1759 and 1765 he published no fewer than 120 articles in *Briefe, die neueste Literatur betreffend* (Letters on the new literature), edited by Nicolai. The circle of savants with whom Mendelssohn held exciting and passionate discourse widened. Of the newcomers his closest acquaintance was Thomas Abbt, a young philosopher and professor of mathematics. Their acquaintanceship began following a warm review by Mendelssohn of an essay by Abbt hailing the patriotism inspired by the war, and Abbt's friendship with Mendelssohn was nourished by a visit to Berlin in the summer of 1761 that was unforgettable for both of them.

In 1763 one of Mendelssohn's essays won first prize in a Royal Academy of Science competition. Assigned to confront the question of whether philosophical truths can furnish the same sorts of evidence as can mathematical truths, he wrote *Abhandlung über die Evidenz in metaphysichen Wissenschaften* (On evidence in metaphysical sciences). In the essay he asserted that philosophy could include genuinely objective arguments, though he acknowledged that such arguments might be more difficult for man to understand than mathematical proofs. Mendelssohn demonstrated his argument by constructing a rational philosophical proof of the existence of God, an argument that would forever remain critical to his philosophy of the Jewish religion. In early June 1763 the members of the Royal Academy of Science committee awarded first prize to Mendelssohn. Immanuel Kant, the philosopher from the University of Königsberg who in the 1780s would inspire a "Copernican revolution" in philosophy, also took part in the competition but received only a commendation. A week later, with unconcealed local and patriotic pride, a Berlin newspaper published the following report: "On Thursday the Royal Academy of Science held its public meeting. The prize was awarded to the local Jew Moses Mendelssohn, who is well known for his writings."

Mendelssohn's rise to prominence as a philosopher was not his only success during the war years. In the summer of 1762, when he was thirty-three, he married Fromet Gugenheim (1737–1812) of Hamburg, and the couple moved into a spacious new home on Spandau Street. In an oft-quoted letter written shortly after the wedding, Mendelssohn told his friend Abbt that the intimate familial experiences of marriage had repressed his passion for philosophizing and diverted his life from its usual course:

> In recent weeks I have neither spoken with nor written to any of my friends. I have stopped thinking, reading, and writing. I have done nothing except delight in happiness, celebrate and observe sacred customs. . . . A blue-eyed maiden whom I now call my wife has caused the ice-cold heart of your friend to melt from emotion, and introduced into his mind thousands of distracting matters from which only now he seeks to gradually free himself.

Mendelssohn spoke of his first meeting with the blue-eyed maiden, in Hamburg in the spring of 1761, as the start of a great love story. For the first time since he had arrived in Berlin in 1747 he left the city to visit his friend Aaron Gumpertz, who was living with a relative, Abraham Gugenheim. At the initiative of Sarah Bernhard, a friend of Fromet Gugenheim's and the daughter of the owner of the silk factory where Mendelssohn worked in Berlin, the two met and fell in love. "The woman I wish to marry has no means, is not beautiful, and is not learned," Mendelssohn informed Lessing on his return to Berlin, minimizing the attributes conventionally sought in a bride, "yet I am a foppish suitor so much in love with her that I believe I can live happily with her." Love at first sight and the notion of happiness as a basis of a marriage were odd criteria for Jews at the time. The historian Jacob Katz contended that the liaison marked a watershed in the evolution of the norms of relations between the sexes in Ashkenazi Jewish society— the emergence of a new erotic ideology. Mendelssohn's visit to Hamburg lasted only four weeks, but the love affair between the two developed rapidly and powerfully, and when they parted Moses took with him the taste of Fromet's kisses. He did not conceal his doubts about arranged matches based upon a financial contract, and for himself demanded the right not only to choose his mate but to forgo the conventional engagement customs, particularly the negotiation of financial arrangements and the ritual exchange of gifts. Mendelssohn based his desire to raise a family with Gugenheim on the deep mutual romantic attraction between them; this was, he emphasized, a personal choice, not a social ritual. In the couple's wedding contract, he stressed, the spoken language was that of the heart. Just as he had taken an unconventional intellectual path after deciding against a rabbinical career, he determined to shape the private, intimate space of his life in accordance with the dictates of his heart.

The couple spent a year apart, beginning in 1761, but remembering Mendelssohn's visit and planning their future nourished their love. Dozens of letters, the majority written in Western Yiddish, were carried by the twice-weekly post coach between Berlin and Hamburg. Most of Mendelssohn's letters have been preserved, but only echoes of Gugenheim's letters survive in the replies of her impatient fiancé. The letters abound with declarations of love, longing, loyalty, and anticipation of their reunion. "My most beloved Fromet" was Mendelssohn's usual salutation. He wrote of the void in his heart that no philosophical study could fill; only her letters, which he read and reread, could console him. The war still raged, and their concerns about it come through in the correspondence. In fact, it was a factor in setting the date of the wedding, along with other logistical issues, like the problem of obtaining a Berlin residency permit for the bride-to-be. Gugenheim's progress in her studies was another frequent topic.

Fromet had been born into a distinguished family with connections to the wealthy elite and the community's leadership; her father, Abraham Gugenheim, was the great-grandson of Samuel Oppenheimer, a well-known court Jew from Vienna. She was educated by private tutors. But from the moment Mendelssohn chose her as his wife, he encouraged her to acquire an education befitting the wife of a philosopher. With Gumpertz supervising her progress, Mendelssohn recommended suitable books and paid for a private French tutor. French was the language of culture in Berlin, and Mendelssohn felt it appropriate that the future lady of the house of a member of the learned elite should be fluent. Was he looking for an intellectual wife? In this regard he seems to have been like other men of the European Enlightenment, who in most respects expected women to conform to their traditional gender role, whose purview was the private space of the home. Despite Mendelssohn's indifference toward convention in choosing his spouse and shaping their emotional relationship, Gugenheim's instruction in languages and literature was designed to prepare her for a role as the philosopher's wife and hostess, not to make her part of the circle of savants in her own right. When it seemed to him that Gugenheim was investing too much effort in her studies, he swiftly set limits appropriate for a woman. It is most important, he wrote her in the early summer of 1761, that she safeguard her health: "Do not harm your body to improve your mind. Study whatever you wish, but in moderation." And in another letter, after six months during which Gugenheim continued to study assiduously, he gently but firmly rebuked and cautioned her:

> What do you seek from this? To become a scholar? God save you from that! Reading in moderation is befitting for women, but not scholarship. A young woman whose eyes are reddened from reading is worthy only of scorn. Fromet, my love, you must find refuge in books but only when you are not in company and seek to amuse yourself, or when you need to read in order to strengthen yourself in the knowledge of good.

This clear gender distinction—the exclusion of women from the world of scholars—is reflected in the earliest preserved portraits of the couple. In a miniature painted on ivory in 1767 Mendelssohn is seen in his study; behind him are crowded bookshelves and the scientific symbols of a globe and skull; he is holding several books, and his finger is inserted between the pages of the top one. He is wearing a thick black house robe, and his sparsely bearded face and big brown eyes display the impatience of a scholar interrupted in his work by the artist; he looks as if he has been forced to close his book for the sitting but will go back to reading it shortly. In Gugenheim's miniature we see a handsome young woman seated in her room in homey restfulness, a married woman's conventional embroidered scarf covering her hair. She wears a necklace, and her apparel has been chosen with care—modest but of high quality. She is seated with her right hand resting on a table covered by a crimson velvet tablecloth on which there is a mirror. Her light-colored eyes display the polite expression of a woman aware of her own worth and conscious of her role as mistress of the house who projects dignity. Their appearance was important to both of them, and in their correspondence before their marriage Gugenheim mentioned the married woman's head covering she was embroidering, and Mendelssohn explained to her why he preferred a wig for a man rather than the troublesome business of haircutting. Only on Sabbaths and festivals did he display his hair, which was usually cared for by a barber; on weekdays he wore a wig, which, he said, saved him energy and cleared his mind for more important matters. Trimming his beard to a thin line running from sideburn to sideburn was another expression of his desire to highlight his uniqueness. The community's religious leadership worried that his tonsorial habits made him look dangerously like a Gentile, but an increasing number of Jewish city dwellers, particularly among the wealthy merchant elite, were adopting this element of the European lifestyle. Fromet Mendelssohn, meanwhile, conformed to the clearly defined roles of housewife, gracious hostess, and devoted family woman, who kept a beautiful home and was fluent in the European languages and literature—in other words, the contemporary European bourgeois ideal of her sex.

Before Gugenheim could leave her parents' home for Berlin, the couple had to obtain a permit to reside in the city, which was hardly keen to accept additional Jews. Mendelssohn's status of "tolerated" Jew in the Prussian kingdom required him to obtain special permission to marry in Berlin. The Hebrew term for a residency permit, *kiyumim* (the right to exist), accurately reflected the Jews' dependence on the rulers' sufferance: in essence, nothing had changed in the legal status of European Jewry. Mendelssohn submitted his request through the leaders of the Jewish community shortly after his return from Hamburg, but the procedure was protracted and strewn with bureaucratic obstacles. In the summer of 1761 Gugenheim started worrying, and Mendelssohn acknowledged: "Fromet, my love, it is not going easily." They would have to wait until the king returned to his winter residence and hope for the goodwill of the chief community leader, Veitel Heine Ephraim. Mendelssohn hinted that the delay was the fault of wealthy Jewish leaders who were unenthusiastic about allowing more Jews to join the community. Once she reached Berlin, he assured her, the couple would avoid the company of those wealthy Jews. Anticipating that this snub might be a source of concern for his wife, he assured her that they would need the company of no one else to be happy. They would be satisfied with each other's company, the romantic wrote in one of his declarations of independence. In the end, Moses and Fromet's home was the focal point of exciting, even tempestuous, social activity throughout their life together; the family rose in Jewish society, they mingled with the wealthy elite, and their children married into it.

After more than six months, on March 26, 1762, Mendelssohn joyfully informed his fiancée: "Yesterday, with God's help, our kiyumim was approved." Now, he added, she was in effect a Prussian subject. However, in this letter, written before the end of the Seven Years' War, this spokesman for the Jewish community who on its behalf had composed anthems lauding the regime and delivered patriotic sermons permitted himself to allude to the country of his residence cynically and mockingly, even with a certain degree of political subversion that sprang from his inferior status as a Jew:

> Now you are a Prussian subject and must support the Prussian side. As a good Prussian you must think only of our good. The Russians, the Turks, the Americans all stand ready to serve us and are only waiting for a wink from us. Our currency is stronger than that of a bank, the whole world seeks security in Berlin, and our bourse is famed from the palace to our home. You must have belief in all this since you now have a kiyumim in Berlin.

In fact, the situation in Berlin was far from stable, and the effects of the war were evident in food shortages and high prices. The population followed the events of the war through the press, and only in the summer, after Russia signed a separate peace treaty with Prussia, were they able to breathe easily. Only then, in early July 1762, some three months after obtaining the residence permit, Gugenheim came to Berlin. The couple married and moved into a two-story house with a back garden at 68 Spandau Street.

To a certain degree, obtaining the kiyumim and marriage license consolidated Mendelssohn's status as a "tolerated" Jew in accordance with the humiliating ranking set out in the 1750 edict. As his fame as a prestigious scholar spread, his friends urged him to exploit it to enhance his legal status, but his self-respect held him back. Mendelssohn did not make a public issue of his aggrievement over the disparity between his prominence as a philosopher and his legal status as a Jew. The matter did, however, surface in private correspondence with his friends and admirers. In April 1762, some two weeks after receiving the kiyumim, he was invited by Isaak Iselin, one of the leaders of the Swiss Enlightenment, to join the Patriotic Society of Bern. Mendelssohn viewed this invitation as a further mark of the esteem he had gained among the luminaries of the European Enlightenment, but with various excuses he tried to wiggle out of accepting it. He explained that his inferior status as a Jew would prevent him from joining an intellectual discourse of political orientation. Although freedom of thought was assured in Friedrich's Prussia, he wrote, "You must surely know what small part the members of my faith have in all the freedoms of this country. The civic oppression to which we are subject due to deep-rooted prejudice lies like a deadweight on the wings of the spirit and prevents any attempt to fly to the heights attained by those who were born free." Only in April 1763, when Fromet was in the eighth month of her first pregnancy, did Mendelssohn agree, out of a sense of responsibility to the family he was building, to swallow his pride and approach Friedrich II with a request for enhanced status and royal protection:

Since my youth I have continuously resided in Your Majesty's domains, and I beg to receive the right of permanent
residency. Although I am an Ausländer and do not possess
the means required by law, I dare to respectfully request that
His Majesty, in his grace, see fit to grant myself and my relatives the protection and freedoms enjoyed by his subjects,
and this in consideration that the shortage of means will be
compensated by my efforts in the sphere of the sciences.

This request, which was written contrary to all of Mendelssohn's principles regarding submissiveness to the sovereign of
the absolutist state, was delivered to the monarch by the king's
confidant Jean-Baptiste Boyer, Marquis d'Argens, the radical
French philosopher who resided in Berlin and was active in the
Royal Academy of Science. Friedrich did not reply. D'Argens,
an admirer of Mendelssohn's who in the past had employed
Aaron Gumpertz, pressed the issue. After a three-month wait
Mendelssohn wrote a second letter, to which the marquis added
an acerbic comment calculated to spur the king to act in accordance with the principle of religious tolerance: "A philosopher who is a poor Catholic [d'Argens] begs from a philosopher
who is a poor Protestant [Friedrich] a privilege for a philosopher who is a poor Jew [Mendelssohn]." Meanwhile, Mendelssohn had won the Royal Academy of Science competition, and
no one in Berlin could ignore his triumph. Finally, in October 1763, the cabinet promoted Mendelssohn up the ladder of
Prussian government rights to the status of *Schutzjude*, "protected Jew."

Despite the civic repression, Mendelssohn's life continued
along the path of success and prestige, the like of which no Jew
of his generation had known. In the seven years between his
marriage and his fortieth birthday, his status as a philosopher
soared, particularly with the publication of his best-selling
Phädon oder über dis Unsterblichkeit der Seele (Phädon; or, on the
immortality of the soul) in 1767. He added further essays to

his corpus, he won the Academy Prize, dignitaries visited his home, his legal status was enhanced, the Berlin Jewish community exempted him from community taxes and recognized him as one of its favorite sons and leading spokesmen, and the Seven Years' War ended and with it a period of anxiety and instability. His family was also growing. In May 1763 Fromet gave birth to their first daughter, who was named after Mendelssohn's mother, Sarah. Sadly, the baby died suddenly before her first birthday. Medicine in Europe was improving, awareness of hygiene was increasing, and life expectancy was on the rise, but infant mortality was still common in the second half of the eighteenth century. Friedrich II himself had succeeded to the throne because two brothers born before him did not reach the age of one year. Three of the Mendelssohn family's children died in infancy, and a fourth, Mendel Abraham, who was named after Mendelssohn's father, died when he was only six.

During this period the sense of familial intimacy became stronger in European society, making parent-child relationships closer than ever before. Mendelssohn approved of this change, and in a letter to his close friend Abbt he proclaimed his sorrow over the tragedy that had beset his house: "Death has knocked at my door and robbed me of a child, which has lived but eleven innocent months; but God be praised, her short life was happy and full of bright promise." Nor had that life been in vain, Mendelssohn wrote, explaining his personal tragedy in his optimistic philosophical terms. Her parents had followed her development from a little animal that wept and slept to the bud of a reasoning creature. "Is no trace of all this left in the whole of nature?" Was it possible that man was ephemeral? Mendelssohn was certain that it was not: "I cannot believe that God has set us on His earth like the foam on the wave," and he found consolation in that thought. From that moment the question of the immortality of the soul became an urgent existential issue, not only a philosophical and religious problem, and he continued with his attempts to find logical proof. *Phädon* was the record of his thoughts on this subject.

If Moses and Fromet Mendelssohn differed from the norms of Jewish marriage in their preference of romance to matchmaking, in at least one respect they were a traditional and conservative couple: they had ten children. Before Sarah died, Fromet was already carrying another daughter; Brendel was born in October 1764. The child grew up in Berlin's haut monde, whose Jewish sons and daughters underwent a profound crisis of identity at the turn of the century. After Mendelssohn's death, Brendel experienced numerous upheavals — besides writing a novel in German, she changed her name to Dorothea, divorced her Jewish husband, lived with and eventually married the Romantic philosopher Friedrich Schlegel, converted first to Protestantism and later to Catholicism. The later trend in her life away from the Enlightenment might have been explained as a romantic rebellion against rationalism, but the veneration of free love and the ultimate turn toward religion could not have been anticipated in the 1760s. In February 1766 the Mendelssohns' first son was born, Chaim, who died after only six weeks. In July 1767 their daughter Recha (Reikel) was born, and in 1769 their son Mendel Abraham, who died, as we have seen, in childhood. Fromet gave birth to five children in the first five years of the marriage, then five more over a little more than another decade: Joseph in 1770, Jente (Henriette) in 1775, Abraham in 1776 (who would become the father of famed composer Felix Mendelssohn-Bartholdy), Sise, who was born in 1778 and died shortly after, and Nathan in 1782. The interval between the births of Joseph and Jente was a consequence of Mendelssohn's illness in the early 1770s. Of the ten children, three sons and three daughters survived their childhood. The parents raised their children lovingly, spending leisure time with them, investing thought and money in their education, and exposing them to the social circles of their parents. When Mendelssohn was away from home, he sent letters full of yearning, love, and kisses to Fromet and the children. The Mendelssohn home was shaped by a combination of tradition and contemporary Berlin bourgeois family life.

"I have a God-fearing wife from a good family," Mendelssohn wrote in a letter to a Jewish friend, proclaiming the traditional elements of his family's life. The family celebrated Sabbaths and festivals, attended synagogue services, and observed the Jewish dietary laws. Mendelssohn had a calendar for the Counting of the *Omer* (the forty-nine days between the second day of Passover and Shavuot), he observed the custom of mourning between the seventeenth day of the Hebrew month of Tammuz and the ninth of Av, he kept his beard, the mark of the traditional Jew, he ensured the religious instruction of his children, and he maintained good relations with the community's rabbis and those of other communities. A magnificently embroidered silk curtain for the Holy Ark, made from Fromet's ornamented wedding gown, was donated by Moses Mendelssohn and his wife to the community synagogue.

At the same time, the family adapted itself to the society of the majority and took part in Berlin's wide range of cultural offerings. Mendelssohn wore wigs, the women of the family dressed in the latest fashion, and their spacious home was furnished as befitted members of the wealthy merchant class. In their salon and garden Moses and Fromet entertained their relatives, Jewish and Christian friends and intellectuals; they were entertained in return, and strolled with their children in the city's parks and along its boulevards. When Solomon Maimon, a young Jew from Lithuania who was to become a renowned philosopher, visited the Mendelssohn home, he felt himself on foreign soil. In his autobiography Maimon wrote: "When therefore I opened dear Mendelssohn's door, and saw him and other respectful people who were there, as well as the beautiful rooms and elegant furniture, I shrank back, closed the door again."

As the Mendelssohns' financial situation improved, further signs of their social standing emerged. The couple employed a cook and servants and hired private tutors to teach their children European languages, providing them a fine musical and literary education as well. Mendelssohn, who was a music lover, attended concerts with his wife and even studied the piano with an eminent Berlin musician. When he fell ill in the 1770s, he twice traveled to the spa at Bad Pyrmont, which was well known not only for its healing properties but also as a resort for German high society. At Pyrmont were boulevards lined with bookshops and cafés, a theater and a dance hall, where one might mingle with scholars and aristocrats, even members of royal families. On one occasion, when Mendelssohn was visiting Königsberg, Fromet sent him a detailed report of what was happening at home. Visitors continued to call, Brendel, who was then thirteen, was practicing her piano pieces, and she herself had gone to the theater. She further wrote:

> On Thursday several good friends called to inquire if I had slept well. In the afternoon Herr Lessing [brother of Gotthold Ephraim Lessing] came and took me, Brendel, and Reikel [who was then eleven] for coffee with his wife, where we found Professor Engel. We had coffee and gossiped about the French theater ensemble and the German theater ensemble. . . . And what do you think we did after coffee, my dear Moses? We foolish women went to the French comedy and the men went to the German ensemble. . . . Brendel understood the plot of the comedy and Reikel will now make every effort to learn and understand, and today at least she is sitting with a French book in her hands.

Reflecting the family's merger of traditional and contemporary experience, the letter, which describes a family deeply involved in the social and cultural life of Berlin, is written in Western Yiddish and is headed, like any letter from the traditional Jewish world: "With God's help, Berlin, the Holy Sabbath Eve, 13 Tammuz 5137."

Mendelssohn's intellectual activities in the 1760s also kept a foot in each world. After his work on the short-lived journal *Kohelet Musar,* he occupied a central position in the enterprise of early maskilim to preserve and renew the tradition of philosophical and scientific study of medieval Jewry. Like Israel Samoscz, Aaron Gumpertz, and other learned men, including Jewish physicians who chafed at the restriction of the Jewish cultural world to the spheres of Torah, Talmud, and Halacha, Mendelssohn worked toward broadening the horizons of knowledge, even among the religious elite, and thus erasing the Jewish community's sense of inferiority in the face of the flourishing of science and philosophy in the Enlightenment culture of Europe. In 1761 Mendelssohn was approached by Samson Kalir, a medical student from Jerusalem who had wandered the communities of Germany and now resided in Berlin under the aegis of the wealthy community leader Veitel Heine Ephraim. Kalir begged him to compose a commentary on Maimonides' *Bi'ur Milot Ha-higayon* (Logical terms). Mendelssohn consented and managed to turn this short twelfth-century treatise — an introduction to logic that had not been reprinted since the 1567 Venice edition — into a kind of textbook for philosophy students.

But Kalir sought to cast himself as the redeemer of Maimonides' book. He printed Mendelssohn's commentary anonymously in Frankfurt an der Oder without the author's knowledge. Mendelssohn suppressed his anger and in 1765 published a new, amended, and expanded edition in Berlin. *Logical Terms,* with Mendelssohn's commentary, was presented as a basic textbook of a text that had been marginalized in Ashkenazi culture: on the one hand it was a rediscovered book by a classic religious author; on the other, the contemporary German commentary reshaped the text in the context of new philosophical terminology and updated anachronistic concepts in the natural sciences and cosmology. Mendelssohn tried to infect students with his great passion for polemics and to defend it against suspicion that "external wisdom" might undermine religious belief. He contended that polemics was actually one of the foundations of the Torah, as its aim was knowledge of God: "The Lord thy God has given Man a heart to know and understand the great and vast and immutable wonders of Creation in order to know His greatness and majesty and to offer thanks for His beneficence which He grants His creatures at every hour and every moment." It is true, he wrote, that human intellect unguided by the Torah and religious tradition was a formula for lost faith. But Torah study supplemented by philosophical and scientific study would produce a faith clear, pure, and free of error.

Mendelssohn called on the young sons of the Jewish scholarly elite to open their eyes to philosophy. A "truth-loving educated man" is one who, along with religious scholarship and faith studies, embraces "inquiry (philosophy) for it to align his intellect and teach him to walk the straight and narrow path and in the circles of justice, and not deviate to the right or left from the path of truth." Those who would reject philosophy as Greek and Aristotelian and therefore alien to Judaism must confront Maimonides' book and its *vade mecum* for the pathways of philosophy, which dispels such suspicion. Logic, Mendelssohn wrote, is like geometry in its neutrality and objectivity; having nothing to do with faith and the commandments, it poses them no threat. No religious stance, no ideas likely to compete with the beliefs and views of traditional Judaism arise from logic, he stressed; it is rather simply an important tool of thinking. It would be appropriate, Mendelssohn recommended, for all young scholars accustomed to devoting all their time to

Torah study to allot an hour or two per week to the study of logic and the basic concepts of philosophy. This renewed connection with Maimonides enabled Mendelssohn to hint in the mid-1760s at his difference with the contemporary rabbinical elite, and at his vision of a philosophical renaissance in Jewish culture—the shaping of an elite which with a basis of Talmudic and Halachic knowledge would incorporate up-to-date scientific and philosophical knowledge and rationalism.

At the same time Mendelssohn was working on the restoration of philosophy in general and medieval Jewish rationalistic thought in particular, he was planning his philosophical masterwork, *Phädon; or, the Immortality of the Soul*. In the early 1760s he became interested in the fourth-century BCE Greek philosopher Plato. As we have seen, he had translated parts of Plato's *The Republic* and also had begun translating into German and revising Plato's renowned treatise *Phaedo*, at the center of which were the dialogues of Socrates with his disciples in prison before he drank from the poisoned chalice. The deaths of Mendelssohn's young children Sarah and Chaim reinforced his conviction that he must deal with the question that troubled, perhaps even frightened him more than any other, a question that held in the balance nothing less than belief in God: is death the absolute loss of being? The positive response of materialist thinkers and scientists, who perceived Man solely as a physiological machine, meant denial of God and of any spiritual essence, demolition of the foundations of human morals. In contrast, a person who believes in an all-merciful, perfect Creator who seeks the best for his creatures must believe also in the intrinsic worth of man above other living creatures, and in man's objective of achieving perfection; such a person must prove to himself that the soul exists and is not destroyed with the death of the body. Mendelssohn dedicated the modern version of *Phädon* to this central existential question, to a philosophical proof that death is not the final word on man.

The book, which first appeared in Berlin in 1767, was a resounding success. The first edition sold out within four months,
further editions were published in 1768, 1769, and 1776, and all
told eleven editions were published in Mendelssohn's lifetime,
an average of one every two years. Additionally, *Phädon* was
translated into Dutch, French, Italian, Danish, Russian, and
Hebrew. The reviewers lavished praise on it, and Mendelssohn
was dubbed "the German Socrates." Readers in Europe were
captivated by the treatise's pleasing literary style, which presented eighteenth-century philosophical ideas in classical form.
Also praised were the dialogues, which portrayed Socrates as
a courageous, moral, and honest philosopher of the Enlightenment fighting for freedom of conscience. Readers credited
Mendelssohn with providing a worthy response to the arguments of the atheists who denied the existence of the soul. An
Enlightenment work, *Phädon* embraced the humanistic ideal of
man as central in the natural world, a thinking, feeling creature
aspiring to perfection and happiness. Writing of the death of
his daughter Sarah, Mendelssohn found unthinkable the notion
that the life of a person was nothing but ephemeral foam on the
waves. It could not be imagined that the "supreme wisdom" that
accorded human beings special qualities and planted in them
the soul, the aspiration to progress from one degree to a higher
one, and the values that motivate human actions—giving a person the impulse, for example, to sacrifice himself for patriotic
or altruistic reasons—would interrupt man's journey toward
perfection, thus making a mockery of his efforts. It is inconceivable, Mendelssohn wrote, that living is the sole aim of life
and that nothing exists beyond it, and it is equally inconceivable
that no explanation and no solution exist for suffering and evil.
A perfect God cannot be hostile to human beings; it is unthinkable that God would seek to harm man or render him an empty
vessel whose every hope is in vain. It is also inconceivable that
the same fate awaits the righteous and evildoers alike. Man's

efforts must continue after death. The consolation of *Phädon* for man in his temporary earthly existence, unlike typical theological consolation with its prescription of religious faith, was grounded in a series of rationalistic philosophical arguments and thus could be accepted by enlightened people in Europe for whom the laws of natural religion were preferable to the dogmas of the Church. Mendelssohn's optimistic assurances of divine providence, of the immortality of the soul, and of man's striving toward perfection provided the believing enlightened with both consolation and rhetorical weapons against both skeptics and heretics.

In contrast with his commentary on *Logical Terms*, intended as a beginners' philosophy textbook for Torah students, *Phädon*, which was written in German, was meant as a general philosophy book. Immediately following its publication, Naphtali Herz Wessely, one of the early maskilim and a Hebrew language scholar, commentator, and poet, proposed translating *Phädon* into Hebrew. In the summer of 1768 the surprised Mendelssohn sent a copy to Wessely in Copenhagen. Mendelssohn admitted that he had not thought Wessely a devotee of philosophy. He wrote that from the outset he had considered writing the book in Hebrew based on treatises written by the Jewish Sages, and apologized for basing his arguments on the immortality of the soul on the Greek Socrates. Wessely, who in the 1780s was to play a key role in the construction of the Jewish Enlightenment's program, told Mendelssohn that he had read *Phädon* in one day, praised him for proving the essence of faith to the general public with "rational proofs," and joined him in the goal of combining religion with wisdom, faith with inquiry. Wessely promised to translate *Phädon* into Hebrew the moment his other commitments allowed it. In the end Wessely did not keep his solemn promise, and the first Hebrew translation appeared only after Mendelssohn's death, but this was the beginning of a friendship between the two men that became stronger when Wessely moved to Berlin a few years later.

Even without a translation of *Phädon*, Hebrew readers became aware of Mendelssohn's ideas on the immortality of the soul through a commentary on Ecclesiastes he wrote between 1768 and 1769. Mendelssohn chose one of the Bible's most notable books of wisdom to revive the medieval tradition of commentary through literality. This also was his first attempt at commentary designed to convey to the contemporary student the content and messages of the ancient text in precise, clear language. Wherever necessary he translated words and idioms into German, just as he did ten years later in his vast exegetic enterprise of translating the Pentateuch. But beyond that his commentary on Ecclesiastes was a treatise on philosophy, ethics, religion, and even modern science through which he conveyed to his Hebrew readers the essence of his worldview and positions—anonymously, as with *Logical Terms* and *Kohelet Musar.* Proving the immortality of the soul was Mendelssohn's primary intellectual mission in the 1760s. In Mendelssohn's view this prime existential question was the key to understanding Ecclesiastes and resolving its ostensible contradictions. Only someone who was convinced of the existence of divine providence, divine justice, and the immortality of the soul could overcome the fear of death and destruction: "For the believer in the existence of God and divine providence cannot escape one or the other—he will either believe that souls live on after death and then will come judgment on every deed whether good or evil, or he will impute, Heaven forfend, injustice and oppression to the Holy God." The commentary of Ecclesiastes is a deep and revealing philosophical-religious discussion of this thorny issue, intended not to raise doubts regarding the value of human life but rather to reinforce belief and hope, and to provide consolation. Mendelssohn not only revealed his philosophical ideas but also adopted the role of the early, moderate Jewish Enlightenment moralist who offered his readers a guide to a harmonious life worthy of man, a life embodying balance between study and thinking, sensuality, aesthetics, pleasure, naturalness, love, and familial warmth, social justice and religious belief.

Through his various works in German and Hebrew, Mendelssohn also nurtured and disseminated at this time an optimistic philosophy lauding man's qualities, the potential of life, and God's grace, which accorded meaning and dignity to the life of the honest man, the family man blessed with intelligence and belief. Had he summed up his social status and literary achievements as he approached the age of forty, he might have been well pleased and satisfied: many sought his friendship, knocked on his door, read his essays, and admired his talents; "the German Socrates" was known afar, the Jewish community basked in the glow of his public prestige, his family grew and was financially sound, and after the death of Isaac Bernhard in 1768, he became the widow Bernhard's partner in the silk business. Yet one of his personal letters reveals that beneath the veneer of harmony and behind the personal and public success, in the hidden backrooms of Mendelssohn's heart gnawed a troubling sense of frustration.

In March 1768 Mendelssohn was approached by Johann Bernhard Basedow, a professor from Altona and a revolutionary thinker in the sphere of education. Basedow, who was later to found in Dessau, the city of Mendelssohn's birth, the Philanthropin—an innovative educational institution in the spirit of Rousseau's natural education—requested his help in promoting his *Elementarwerk*, a moderate Enlightenment call for educational reform. In the author of the much-admired *Phädon* he hoped to find a kindred spirit and a spiritual leader of the Jews who would be able to collect subscribers in Berlin to purchase his book. Mendelssohn's reply again gave vent to his bitter and

angry consciousness of his civic situation as a Jew in Prussia—
a self-awareness in stark contrast with the optimistic messages
of his published works at the time. If Basedow believed that
his book and educational programs were suitable for the Jews,
Mendelssohn wrote, he must be unaware of their situation:
"The nobler your intentions, the wiser your principles and the
means you seek to adopt more correct, thus our ability to make
use of them is lessened." Basedow's programs were conceived
to educate intelligent, law-abiding, and humane human beings,
lovers of truth and liberty who serve their country, Mendelssohn wrote, but the Jews could not be part of this ideal:

> Should [the Jew] learn to respect human rights? If the Jew
> does not want to become even more wretched under civic op-
> pression, it would be better if he did not know of these rights.
> Must he love truth and the freedom that is in intelligence to
> reach despair? For all the civil arrangements in many places
> are in fact intended to distance him from these two things!
> And must he be willing to serve his country? The only ser-
> vice the country receives from him is money. Payment of
> high taxation under conditions of restricted livelihood is the
> only vocation that my brethren need to be able to fill.

With a measure of cynicism Mendelssohn added, "When your
Elementarwerk teaches this science, then my people will welcome it for they have no need of anything else." The gap between the restricted status of the Jews of Europe and the innovations of Enlightenment culture seemed to Mendelssohn to be
so deep, injurious, and intolerable that Jews would be better off
shielded from that culture in order to minimize their wretched-
ness and frustration.

The contradiction between the humanistic values of Enlightenment culture and the civic oppression to which the Jews
were subject continued to trouble Mendelssohn even at the
peak—in fact, to call that success into question. As long as Jews

were subject to restrictions and discrimination, how could they identify with the sublime values of the Enlightenment whose banner Mendelssohn bore? He concluded his letter to Basedow with a familiar attempt at repression: "But enough of all that, these thoughts depress me to the point that I am unable to think about this without a sense of revulsion." But that frustration inevitably resurfaced, barely a year later. At the end of the summer of 1769 an unexpected episode deepened that frustration and compelled Mendelssohn to deal, for the first time in the public arena, with the question of his dual identity—that of the Enlightenment philosopher and Jew.

5

Affront and Sickness: The Lavater Affair

FOR FIFTEEN years Mendelssohn delineated a protected social space for himself. In a political, civil, and economic milieu
riddled with suspicion, oppression, and hostility toward Jews,
he crafted a standing of respect in the community of scholars
and men of letters. Personal friendship was the bulwark of this
status, almost a ritual of eighteenth-century Germany, where
men of the intellectual elite readily displayed their feelings publicly. His friendships, founded on mutual respect and trust, were
nurtured in groups, in reciprocal visits, and in correspondence,
reassuring Mendelssohn that there existed a territory in which
he could enjoy equality, freedom, and respect—and immunity
from prejudice, discrimination, and persecution. In October
1769, though, Johann Caspar Lavater breached the walls of this
protected space, brutally trampled the ideals of friendship, and
challenged Mendelssohn's status as a citizen of the enlightened
community, leaving him insulted, indignant, betrayed.

Lavater, a Zurich clergyman who belonged to the enlightened circles of Europe and whose study of physiognomy—assessment of character and personality according to facial features—had found many admirers, visited Mendelssohn in Berlin several times in the course of 1763–1764. Like many other visitors, Lavater, then only twenty-two years old, was immensely impressed by the Jewish philosopher, held numerous discussions with him in his parlor and his office at the silk factory, and forged a friendship with him. In their last conversation Lavater pressed Mendelssohn to reveal his views on Christianity. Mendelssohn reconstructed their friendly conversation thus:

> It seems you still recollect the confidential conversation I had the pleasure of holding with yourself and your worthy friends in my apartment. Can you then possibly have forgotten how frequently I sought to divert the discourse from religious to more neutral topics, and how much yourself and your friends had to urge me before I would venture to deliver my opinion on a subject of such vital importance?

After receiving assurances that no public use would be made of anything he said, Mendelssohn was prepared to state with extreme caution that although he had little direct knowledge of Christianity, he bore no animus toward Christians and respected the morality of Jesus' character. Mendelssohn's declaration was consistent with the contemporary trend of tolerance toward Christians to which several rabbis, including Rabbi Jacob Emden, subscribed. But Mendelssohn was unaware of Lavater's intense eschatological and millenarian agenda. On the one hand, like the devout of the "religious enlightenment," he advocated a Christianity founded on science and reason, but on the other he shared the expectations, widespread in the eighteenth century, of Christians who dreamed of the messianic Kingdom of the Millennium. In a book published in 1768, Lavater explicitly states: "I am deeply convinced that the imminently expected Millennium will not occur before the entire Jewish nation has converted to Christianity, or at least that the beginning of the Thousand-year Kingdom of Christ is directly linked to a general conversion of the Jews."

Five years after that conversation Mendelssohn received by mail a copy of *Philosophical and Critical Inquiries Concerning Christianity*, a newly published and as yet unbound book by Charles Bonnet, a naturalist and philosophical writer from Geneva, that had been translated into German by Lavater. Bonnet's work held less interest for Mendelssohn than did Lavater's preface, where, on the first page, the translator in effect publicly challenged the "German Socrates," anticipating nothing less than his conversion to Christianity:

> The amiable discretion with which, notwithstanding your contrariety to the Christian religion, you delivered your opinion on it, is still fresh in my memory. And so indelible and important is the impression, which your truly philosophical respect for the moral character of its Founder made on me, in one of the happiest moments of my existence, that I venture to beseech you—nay, before the God of truth, your and my creator and father, I beseech and conjure you—to read this work, I will not say, with philosophical impartiality, which I am confident will be the case, but for the purpose of publicly refuting it, in case you should find the main arguments, in support of the facts of Christianity, untenable; or, should you find them conclusive, with the determination of doing what policy, love of truth, and probity demand—what Socrates would doubtless have done, had he read the work, and found it unanswerable.

In this act of Lavater's, Friedrich Nicolai, one of Mendelssohn's close friends, identified the messianic fervor that drove him. To Nicolai it was clear that Lavater had exploited Mendelssohn's private approval of Jesus' moral character to embark upon an ambitious course that would commence with the conversion to Christianity of the renowned philosopher from Berlin, continue with multitudes of Jews following in his footsteps, and culminate in the Thousand-year Kingdom. Mendelssohn was furious. The preface appeared in every copy of the German translation; it could not be ignored. The community of scholars now anticipated Mendelssohn's response to the patently obvious challenge—could the Jewish philosopher deny philosophical arguments in favor of Christianity? Would he engage in a theological debate against Christianity? Would he relinquish his Judaism? Mendelssohn asked himself and his friends what had motivated Lavater to set such a trap; was this the price of friendship? Mendelssohn fully understood the significance of the public challenge: he was facing a test of his Enlightenment and of the entire enlightened community. Lavater had breached the lines between the country's political-judicial arena, where Mendelssohn, like all his brethren, suffered inferior status and civic oppression; the theological arena, with its mutual age-old hostility between Christians and Jews; and the new and seemingly protected arena of men of culture and letters, where religious tolerance and social equality were supposed to prevail. Mendelssohn's fury, though, was first and foremost personal, born of Lavater's betrayal of trust:

> It might have been reasonably inferred that a public rehearsal of the earlier discussion would be extremely repugnant to my disposition; and that I must have inevitably become the more embarrassed. . . . What then, sir, could induce you to single me thus, against my well-known disinclination, out of the many, and force me into a public arena, which I so much wished never to have occasion to enter?

In the fifteen years of his developing career as a philosopher Mendelssohn had managed to maintain separation between the public arena, in which he acted as a renowned Enlightenment philosopher, and his private space as a Jew, a family man and member of the community and the synagogue. Lavater's blatant and embarrassing challenge turned Mendelssohn's Judaism, too, into a public issue and a subject for public discussion.

For about two and a half months Mendelssohn deliberated on how to respond—should he embark on a personal attack against Lavater's messianic and missionary pretensions or refute Bonnet's evidence in the very public arena where Lavater had issued his challenge? Refutation was not a particularly difficult task, and he had already drafted his arguments in favor of the absolute preeminence of Judaism over Christianity. One of the most scathing sentences he wrote in anger caustically condemned the persecution countenanced by Christianity: "The fact that the small, despised and scattered group of Jews still exists can be credited to a humanist theologian, may his ashes be blessed, who was the first to proclaim that God keeps us as living proof of the truth of Christianity. Were it not for this brilliant notion, we would have been obliterated long ago." Meanwhile Mendelssohn had gained an important new Christian ally: Karl Wilhelm Ferdinand, crown prince of the Duchy of Braunschweig. In 1769 Ferdinand, nephew of Friedrich II, a general who had distinguished himself in the Seven Years' War, and a lover of science and culture, visited Berlin and invited Mendelssohn for a talk at the palace. The royal honor conferred upon Mendelssohn was reported in a Berlin newspaper, and the crown prince's declared intention to maintain close contact with the philosopher was the subject of more than one exchange of letters in the community of scholars. For Mendelssohn Ferdinand's attention was proof that Lavater's clumsy effort had not undermined his status, and that a considered and astute response to the ultimatum was more appropriate than an antagonistic one.

He decided to draft an open letter to Lavater that would publicly reveal the injustice perpetrated against him. On December 12, 1769, he finished his *Schreiben an den Herrn Diaco-*

nus Lavater zu Zürich (Letter to Deacon Lavater of Zurich), a short essay that became one of his most important and celebrated texts to date. Despite its extremely personal context, this essay became the Enlightenment philosopher's main text in support of religious tolerance. This subject, which was of cardinal importance in European Enlightenment, had long been an existential question for Mendelssohn—recall his publication against Michaelis in 1754—upon which depended both his personal status and the fate of the Jews. In Mendelssohn's view, the Lavater affair only heightened the importance of safeguarding the value of religious tolerance. Mendelssohn's simple tactics brought him public support and admiration. Instead of responding directly to the either/or ultimatum—refuting Bonnet's evidence or converting to Christianity—Mendelssohn explained why interdenominational disputation intrinsically ran counter to the values of Enlightenment culture, and why Lavater's ultimatum was an unfair gesture contrary to the values of friendship.

The main argument of the "Letter to Deacon Lavater" is that interdenominational polemics is completely one-directional since unlike Christianity, Judaism does not claim exclusivity and is not a missionary religion. The laws of the Torah handed down to the Jews on Mount Sinai are binding solely upon the Jews. The rabbis do not encourage proselytizing and take pains to explain to would-be converts to Judaism the difficulties involved in observance of the religious precepts and in joining a nation subject to humiliation and oppression. Moreover, Mendelssohn wrote, while the Christian church declares that there can be no redemption outside it, Judaism grants the divine reward promised to the Jews to anyone observing "the Seven Commandments of Noah" or the Noahide Laws—laws prohibiting idolatry, incest, bloodshed, and robbery, proscriptions compatible with general humanist moral teachings: "All who conduct their lives in accordance with this religion of nature and reason are the righteous of the nations and have a share in the world to come." Mendelssohn based this key concept on Talmudic and rabbinic sources, enlisted as well ideas he found in the words of Rabbi Jacob Emden, and relied finally on Maimonides' phrasing. He rejected, however, Maimonides' distinction, which from his standpoint was problematical, between the non-Jew who observed the Noahide Laws out of duty and obedience to the divine commandment (and would thus be worthy of the title "righteous of the nations" and gain his just reward) and those who did so after deliberation (whose religious status Maimonides deemed inferior).

This was the first time that Mendelssohn expressed the view that different faiths share a common basis in a natural religion that has no need of revelation or scriptures. He even contended that Judaism, because it does not zealously observe the principle of exclusivity and preeminence, is the closest to natural religion and also the most tolerant. According to Mendelssohn, Judaism is the only religion that resolves the tension between universality and exclusivity, between man as man and the cultural diversity of nations and religions. While the unique qualities of Judaism set it apart from other creeds, he continued, it recognizes the philosophical and historical legitimacy of all the monotheistic religions. These qualities accord Judaism a place of honor in Enlightenment culture, while the missionary fervor of Christians places them in an absurd light as people who reject tolerance and freedom of opinion and religion, who act contrary to reason. Mendelssohn explained the folly of Lavater's challenge:

> Suppose there were living among my contemporaries a Confucius or a Solon, I could, according to the principles of my faith, love and admire the great man without falling into the ridiculous idea that I must convert a Solon or a Confucius. Convert him? Why? Because he is not a member of the Jew-

ish faith? He is not subject to the laws of my religion, and in the matter of doctrines we shall quickly reach agreement. Do I not believe that he can dwell in the world to come? I think that a man who guides others in the ways of charity in this world cannot be an inheritor of hell in the next.

The universal and humanistic religious approach of natural religion, which had gained renown for the author of *Phädon*, was now presented as the basic approach of Judaism.

Unlike his philosophical treatises, but like some of his personal letters, the "Letter to Deacon Lavater" contains numerous personal expressions and further reveals Mendelssohn's distress and frustration. Even though his argument was restrained, it scarcely concealed the agitation of a Jew who found himself extremely vulnerable. Mendelssohn expressed awareness of his weakness as a Jew in the confrontation with Lavater—the position of inferiority that ostensibly was solely theoretical and academic, but which in fact upset the order of his life. First he challenged Lavater—and through him all the members of the enlightened scholarly community who were following the debate—to acknowledge Mendelssohn's intellectual occupation as a philosopher to be free of any vested interests and tendentiousness. As a Jew, he wrote, his hands were tied, and so it was unfair to urge him to reveal his views on Christianity in public. "In the situation in which I found myself I could not expect that the sciences would invent any kind of favor for me in this world," he wrote. "I knew full well," he went on, underscoring the restrictions that prevented him from making a living in the academy or the civil service, "that a living or success could never be for me in this way." And what of the enjoyment and satisfaction in the philosophical knowledge of the basic humanistic values of the Enlightenment? In this regard Mendelssohn replied in a similar spirit to Basedow: "And pleasure? O, my most worthy lover of Man! The situation imposed on my brethren of my faith in civil life is so remote from the free use of the powers of the soul that none of our people can gain satisfaction in the knowledge of human rights from their true aspect." The awareness of the enlightened Jew of the disjunction between the "human rights" slogans of the Enlightenment and their own civil oppression causes more frustration than enjoyment, Mendelssohn wrote. Even knowing the extent to which Judaism was debased, he could not aspire to defend its honor by means of polemical confrontation. Even in discerning "among my civil colleagues national prejudices and distorted religious views," he imposed silence upon himself, and in order not to seem ungrateful did not attack the ruling nation that granted nominal protection and freedom of religious practice to Jews. Here Mendelssohn's emotions burst out in a painful and trenchant complaint against the injustice of trampling the natural rights of the Jews underfoot:

> I am a member of an oppressed people which must appeal to the benevolence of the government for protection and shelter, and nowhere do I receive them unless it is within the known restrictions. The freedoms permitted to all men, the members of my faith willingly relinquish, and they are happy that they are tolerated and protected. They must be grateful to the nation that receives them under bearable conditions and consider this as considerable grace, since in several countries they are even prevented from holding the right of thought. Even under the laws of the city of your birth your circumcised friend is not even allowed to visit you in Zurich! And how grateful must my brethren be to the ruling nation, which embraces them within the general love of humankind and allows them to freely worship their God in accordance with the custom of their forefathers? In the country in which I reside they enjoy, from that point of view, the fairest of freedom, so should they disagree with the religion of the majority?

In Mendelssohn's opinion, these special circumstances of civic oppression and the special protection of the Prussian kingdom mandated great caution. However, to remove all doubt that the "Letter" was not an attempt to evade Lavater's ultimatum, he also declared his unshakable loyalty to the Jewish faith, even though it, too, was not free of superstition and hypocrisy to which a seeker of the truth like himself found it difficult to reconcile himself:

> I am completely convinced of the immutability of my religion as you or M. Bonnet are sure of yours, and I hereby attest before the God of Truth, the Creator who sustains you and me . . . that I shall continue to hold my beliefs for as long as my soul does not change its nature. The distance from your religion, of which I informed you and your friends, has not lessened since then.

Mendelssohn added that his true Christian friends were those who allowed him to maintain his position in the learned community, distinguishing between faith and philosophy: "We love one another truly although we do assume that in matters of faith and religion our views are divided." Among these enlightened friends not one would conceive of converting the other, and anyone thinking like Lavater that Bonnet's arguments for the virtues of Christianity were irrefutable would in fact remove himself from the ranks of enlightened people aspiring to the truth, by virtue of an inability to dissociate himself from his negative preconceptions of Judaism. In a sarcastic aside Mendelssohn wrote: "One of us is surely a shining example of the power of the education and prejudices to rule even those people who seek to know the truth with an unblemished heart." In Mendelssohn's opinion, Lavater suffered a resounding failure in these Enlightenment tests. "Whoever believes that outside his house of prayer a man cannot attain eternal happiness," he wrote, has removed himself from the Enlightenment camp and

joined that of the religious fanatics, the dogmatists, the misan-
thropists, those possessed by the lust for persecution, the in-
decent betrayers of their friends.

The confrontation forced upon Mendelssohn by Lavater
became a stormy affair that engaged public opinion for more
than two years. In the community of scholars and writers in
the German-speaking countries everyone was curious to read
everything that had been written in the course of the affair,
and everyone sought his colleagues' opinions. Beginning early
in 1770, Lavater's and Mendelssohn's writings were reprinted,
pamphlets were published, articles appeared in journals, and
the men's respective views were debated in the correspondence
of intellectuals. Lessing, Nicolai, Michaelis, Herder, Johann
Georg Hamann, and other philosophers all expressed their
opinions. There was no consensus on the matter, and the very
fact of public engagement encouraged a polemical response
from Christian religious fanatics, but in the end Mendelssohn
was satisfied with the tenor of public opinion. Most commentators agreed that Lavater's ultimatum had been rash, insen-
sitive, discourteous, and hurtful, and that Mendelssohn's response had been dignified and admirable. Bonnet, whose book
had sparked the controversy, wrote to Mendelssohn that the
preface had been composed without his knowledge and that
he deplored Lavater's exploitation of the forum. He emphasized as well that his treatise had not been directed at the Jews.
Mendelssohn replied immediately: "In what a happy world we
would live if all men accepted and practiced the truth which the
best Christians and the best Jews commonly possess."

However, Mendelssohn remained on the defensive. Even
his friends and supporters exerted polite pressure on him—
perhaps he would still be willing to explain not only why he rejected an interfaith debate but also how such a debate contradicted Christian ideals as well. Prince Karl Wilhelm Ferdinand
of Braunschweig, for example, after reading the "Letter to Dea-

con Lavater" begged Mendelssohn in a short letter written on January 2, 1770, to reveal his opinions: "There is nothing of greater importance to a man of our religion than to see how a philosopher who lives in the Jewish religion believes in the historical paragon of Moses, in which we are in agreement with him, and how he still evades the historical proofs on which the Christian faith is founded." Still moved by the crown prince's friendship and grateful for the unprecedented meeting between them in the palace in Berlin, Mendelssohn broke his customary silence. Requesting that his reply not be publicized, he told Ferdinand what he truly thought about Christianity. First, he argued, the divine perception of Christianity—belief in the Holy Trinity and divine incarnation in Jesus—contradicted reason and could not be true. In his opinion, these principles "diametrically oppose the fundaments of human knowledge. According to my cognizance I cannot equate them with what I have been taught by reason and study of the thinking of the nature of the divinity and its qualities, and I am compelled to reject them." Even Reform Christianity, which relegated Jesus to the rank of an ordinary mortal, viewing him only as God's emissary and prophet, would have to face several tests before a Jew like Mendelssohn could relate to it positively. It would have to relinquish its claim to exclusivity as the true religion ("it is inconceivable that a religion that makes others separate could be a true religion"); abandon the doctrines of eternal damnation and original sin, as well as belief in Satan and evil spirits; and finally, recognize that Jesus did not demand the annulment of the Law of Moses or exempt believers from observing its commandments. Only under these terms—which, practically speaking, would negate the dogma of Christianity—"would a religion be attained in which Christians and Jews could participate equally."

In reply to the crown prince's question of how Mendelssohn dealt with the Christological proofs of the Christian truths embodied in the Old Testament, he could scarcely conceal his derision. He contended that all the verses serving as evidence of the truths of Christianity and heralding its appearance before Jesus' time were either erroneous interpretations or maliciously misleading. "How wretched the fate of men would be," Mendelssohn remarked cynically, "were the eternal happiness of the entire human race to depend on an interpretation of nebulous places of a book written at the dawn of history in a foreign tongue, which today is dead, for a particular people in Asia!" Fearful that his frankness might offend the crown prince, Mendelssohn concluded with a request "of His Highness to destroy this letter lest it fall into the hands of those who might make ill use of it, or by virtue of his position see himself bound to incite strife and contention." If published, this confession doubtless would have fueled the flames of the Lavater affair. The words of Mendelssohn, the Jewish philosopher accepted by the enlightened community, reveal that he shrank from Christianity, viewed it as a religion of error and deception, and believed it to contradict the Enlightenment and run counter to truth and reason. Unlike Lavater, though, the crown prince upheld the principle of friendship, and the public remained ignorant, for a time, of what the "German Socrates" really thought about Christianity.

Mendelssohn was part of another confidential correspondence during those January days. The eschatological vision that Lavater attempted to promote included, as conditions for the realization of the Thousand-year Kingdom, not only the Jews' conversion to Christianity but also their return to the Land of Israel. Graf Rochus Friedrich zu Lynar, a German statesman employed by various European royal courts, approached Mendelssohn anonymously with a request for his opinion on a plan to establish a state for the Jews in the Land of Israel. Mendelssohn's reply to the "esteemed gentleman" was utterly negative—just as the Jews' conversion should not be expected, their return to their historical home was impractical and inconceivable. For Mendelssohn, not only did "such a daring enterprise" face vast difficulties of implementation both economic and political, but the Jewish nation lacked the collective willpower for such an initiative. Throughout his life, while Mendelssohn chafed against civil oppression and worked toward building a civil society in which Jews could live in dignity, he never aligned himself with any enterprise devoted to a national rebirth for Jews living in exile. He felt that the Jewish Diaspora was distanced from politics and the world of action, and in large part even bereft of the natural aspiration to freedom:

> It is not overly ready to attempt something grandiose. The pressure under which we have been living for so many centuries has removed any vitality from our spirit. This is not our fault, but we cannot deny that the natural instinct for freedom has subdued the energy for action in us. It has become the alms of monks, and is manifested in prayer and suffering and not in action.

And in any case, Mendelssohn hinted, he was not the right man for practical ideas. Public opinion increasingly portrayed him as the leading representative of Judaism, but he strove to define his talents within the borders of his beloved philosophy. "My valor, if indeed I possess such a thing," Mendelssohn noted in a letter to Lynar, "is limited to purely speculative matters. In practical matters I have always been restricted to a most limited sphere that is beyond my ability to acquire the industry to rise to great enterprises."

From a letter he wrote to Avigdor Levi, a young private tutor from the Prague community, we can also appreciate his weariness of the debate with Lavater and his ambivalence about having been in the front line of public opinion. Mendelssohn tells Levi of the pressure he had been under since the affair began: "I have fallen into the pit of the debate with a clergyman of the Christian faith" after carefully avoiding all inter-religious controversy throughout his life, he wrote, and, having responded to Lavater's challenge, he had been assailed from every direction by "all the people of that faith and those who support it have encircled me, this one wrathfully, that one with honeyed and smooth words, another angrily and yet another laughingly, for this is their way, and in any event they trouble me with their words and dreams. And I have placed my trust in God my fortress, He will gird me for His battle and give me the words to utter, and I shall know that I will not be ashamed."

Mendelssohn's low spirits when he wrote to Levi stemmed from the recent publication of one of the bitterest anti-Jewish responses in the course of the affair. Johann Balthasar Kölbele, a Frankfurt jurist, attacked not only the "Letter to Deacon Lavater" but also Jews in general, claiming that Mendelssohn either was a heretic or was concealing the threadbare clothing of a traditional rabbi beneath his fashionable apparel. Kölbele was censured from all sides for his diatribe, but Mendelssohn began to imagine himself in the eye of the storm of a large-scale attack on Judaism.

Meanwhile, Lavater wrote a letter begging Mendelssohn's forgiveness and at the same time prepared his public response to the "Letter to Deacon Lavater," which he hoped might restore the blighted friendship. The publication in April 1770 of the response, to which was appended an epilogue by Mendelssohn, somewhat cooled the public dispute between the two. Lavater's *Antwort an den Herrn Moses Mendelssohn zu Berlin* (Reply to Herr Moses Mendelssohn in Berlin) mollified Mendelssohn to some extent, since it included a public request for forgiveness and an expression of apology for the mistake he had made in present-ing his ultimatum in the preface to Bonnet's book: "I hereby retract my earnest demand, which I had insufficient right to make, and publicly and with all my heart beg you: forgive me for my exaggerated entreaty, for the irreparable damage in my

preface. . . . It will be hurtful to me should I have unintention-
ally caused you any distress by not devoting sufficient thought
to your situation." Lavater, however, neither abandoned his far-
reaching vision of conversion nor eased his pressure on Mendelssohn, and asked him how, as a philosopher, he dealt with
the irrefutable proofs of the verity of Christianity. While ac-
knowledging that his tactics may have been inappropriate, he
declared himself still unable to understand what philosophical
underpinnings might justify continued adherence to Judaism.
Paradoxically, having just expressed remorse for the way he had
addressed Mendelssohn in the preface, Lavater wrote candidly
that his principal aim was to serve the Christian faith, in part
by bringing all his friends, including Mendelssohn, to happiness and truth. He wrote that although part of Mendelssohn's
response had melted his heart and brought tears to his eyes, he
still imagined that his heart's desire would be fulfilled. "How I
wish you were a Christian!" he wrote, and concluded with the
words: "I shall never be able to relinquish my hope of finding
you, if not now, then surely in the future, among the happy admirers of Him, whose patrimony is the community of Jacob,
of my Lord and Master Jesus of Nazareth, may His name be
praised for ever and ever, Amen!"

In his response Mendelssohn chose to ignore Lavater's blunt
missionary leanings, and in the "Epilogue to the Response to
Herr Moses Mendelssohn in Berlin by Johann Caspar Lavater"
he sought to end this embarrassing public dispute on a conciliatory note. Mendelssohn heaped praise on Lavater's character,
contended that he had never been insulted, and admitted that
the episode had been the occasion of increased understanding
for his stance against any interreligion confrontation. To the
debate itself he added his opinion (which he later developed
in his *Jerusalem*) that Judaism does not accept miracles as evidence of religious truth, and is based upon adherence to the
commandments—revealed divine law. Mendelssohn devoted a

particularly sharp and critical portion of the epilogue to a contemptuous rejection of Kölbele's anti-Jewish attitude, attrib-
uting it to a distorted picture of Judaism taken from Johann
Eisenmenger's notorious early-eighteenth-century book *Ent-
decktes Judentum* (Judaism unmasked). There can be no doubt
that Mendelssohn was relieved that the debate—and the public treatment of his private life—had come to an end: "I am
pleased that Herr Lavater has willingly agreed to end the public correspondence." He was uncomfortable in the limelight
and felt it inappropriate that discourse of this kind should be
held before an audience: "Why should we make the audience a
witness to such negotiations? It is unfair to both Herr Lavater
and myself to make ourselves the butt of spectacles among the
idlers in the audience, to arouse resentment among the weak
and provide an opportunity for evil enjoyment to those who
treat truth and good with contempt." Accepting at face value
Lavater's desire to restore their friendship to its former footing, Mendelssohn was more concerned about removing the
subject from the agenda as quickly as possible. He would, he
declared, ignore any further challenges, criticism, and denials
pertaining to the affair, at least "until I am sure that I shall
be unable to use my time for a greater purpose than this." He
had no illusions about any abatement in Lavater's missionary
zeal or the hostility of Christians like Kölbele who might yet
use the episode to encourage dangerous anti-Jewish sentiment.
"In the few hours of rest my occupation affords me," he wrote
in the epilogue, "I long to forget all the schisms, all the strife,
which has lately made Man the enemy of Man, and endeavor
to erase from my memory all the attempts that assail me in the
course of the day." As in other instances, Mendelssohn could
experience total freedom only in thought, in philosophy. He
was not, he suspected, the right man to prosecute such public
battles as the Lavater affair. Three years before the affair began,
before the wave of adulation that *Phädon* brought, Mendels-

sohn had toyed with the idea of leaving Berlin and his position at the silk factory and settling in a smaller Jewish community, far from the limelight, in order to devote his life to science and philosophy. In a personal letter to Nicolai he wrote of the desire to sequester himself within the four walls of a private scholar and of the great effort he had to invest in other activities; he tortured himself, he wrote, with self-criticism for being insufficiently resolute and decisive: "I wish I were able to sacrifice more for the advancement of my leanings towards science. The talent of deciding, the talent of deciding! That is what I am missing constantly."

Mendelssohn was buoyed by several supportive responses to his "Epilogue," including one from his former adversary Michaelis, who had become an enthusiastic supporter. He found further consolation, too, in the bosom of his family, which in August 1770 was joined by Joseph, who would become the first son to reach adulthood. Two months later Mendelssohn was thrilled when the Crown Prince of Braunschweig invited him for a visit to continue the conversation that had begun in Berlin and continued in their correspondence. In October 1770 Mendelssohn left Berlin for the first time in nine years and traveled to Braunschweig on a short visit. He was warmly welcomed by the prince and the duchess, the sister of Friedrich II, and spent many hours in their company. His journey was a particularly happy one because he also visited his old friend Lessing, who was chief librarian at the Herzog-August Bibliothek in Wolfenbüttel.

When he returned to Berlin in early November, Mendelssohn gave his friends an enthusiastic account of his visit with the erudite, tolerant prince who supported the Enlightenment, but in a personal letter he again revealed the rage seething within. Writing to his relative Elkan Herz, who resided in Leipzig and had followed the Lavater affair, he gave voice to acerbic comments that could not be uttered in public, and that contradicted his stated desire to leave the debate behind him. In the 1770s there were still no forums for the expression of Jewish public opinion, yet voices of Jews had reached Mendelssohn, pleaded that he withdraw from the debate to avoid rousing anti-Jewish sentiment. "You ask me why I allowed myself to become involved in this debate," he wrote to Herz in a bellicose tone that was barely expressed in his written public responses; "how I wish I were even more deeply involved." He had no regrets, he added, and paid no heed to the slanders against him. The implication is clear that he had withdrawn from the debate under pressure, and that he remained keen to give public expression to his criticism of Christianity, which so far had appeared only in his letter to the Prince of Braunschweig. Decrying Jews unnerved by every Jewish voice raised in public, he went on in his letter to Herz, "I do not understand at all how so many of our faithful friends are always shouting that for Heaven's sake I should not write any further on this subject." Mendelssohn was affronted, frustrated, and angry, but he felt that his hands were tied, and so had agreed to declare his part in the debate closed: "God knows that I was not happy to end the debate . . . and if it were up to me I would have given a completely different response."

Aftereffects of the Lavater affair dragged on, much to the public distress of Mendelssohn, yet he still harbored the argumentative instinct to put Lavater to rout. In January 1771 he was compelled to continue his correspondence with Lavater, refuting charges that had appeared in anonymous pamphlets that the Jews despised Jesus; again he expressed his hope that enlightened people from both religions would prevail over prejudiced clerics and put an end to religious persecution and hatred.

In early February 1771 his frustration was exacerbated anew. Members of the Royal Academy of Science elected him a fellow in its company of philosophers, the greatest honor imaginable for an eighteenth-century Prussian scholar. The only known precedent of an appointment of this kind for a Jew had occurred in London during the same period, when the Sephardi scholar Emanuel Mendez da Costa was elected fellow of the Royal Society of London. Mendelssohn's election in Berlin constituted official recognition of his standing in the scholarly establishment. Johann Georg Sulzer informed Mendelssohn of the election in a formal letter and requested his acceptance of the honor, which at this stage would include no remuneration but gave him hope that in the future he might be appointed a salaried fellow and thus be freed of the burden of earning a living. But Friedrich II balked at the official appointment of the Jew Mendelssohn as a member of the Prussian scholarly establishment. The Academy's decision required royal approval, but such approval was not forthcoming, even though in September 1771 the Academy again ratified Mendelssohn's election. In the wake of Lavater's betrayal, the anti-Jewish writings that had been disseminated during the affair, and Mendelssohn's exposure to the clerics' missionary zeal, the king's deafening silence drew a clear border that the Jew was precluded from crossing. Mendelssohn tried to console himself and his friends by saying that the election by the academics was far more important than the king's rejection, but the disappointment was another bitter reminder of contrast between the civic repression he suffered and the academic acclaim he received.

During the tense weeks of waiting for Friedrich II's approval, Mendelssohn was afflicted by a mysterious illness, probably arrhythmia. Suddenly his work was halted for a year and a half. In his first attack of palpitations one March night, Mendelssohn awoke in alarm with a feeling of paralysis and suffocation; thereafter the attacks recurred after any physical or intellectual effort. These symptoms of heart disease were not fully understood by eighteenth-century medicine, and Mendelssohn's eminent Jewish physician, Markus Bloch, a member of the Naturalist Society of Berlin, diagnosed his illness as congestion of blood in the brain brought on by mental stress. Another well known practitioner, Johann Georg Zimmermann, who was a court physician in Hanover, confirmed this diagnosis, and the two agreed on a series of aggressive treatments to slow the flow of blood and prevent any excitement and effort: mustard plasters, bleeding, leeches, baths, and strict instructions for diet. Mendelssohn was ordered to abstain from meat, tobacco, coffee—which he particularly liked—and alcoholic beverages. This treatment appears to have physically weakened Mendelssohn even further and caused him depression. For several months he lacked the strength to climb the stairs to his study on the second floor of his home. Particularly severe was the physicians' order to completely suspend all intellectual activity, because conversation, reading, and writing were thought to stimulate circulation. So from March 1771 to the summer of 1772, Mendelssohn barely left his home, absenting himself for many months from the silk factory, receiving only a few visitors in his salon, reading and studying only a bit, and writing few letters—only some twenty letters from this period have been preserved, compared with the scores he customarily wrote each year. He devoted most of his time to his treatments and diet, and to his family. His family also ceased to grow because of the physical restrictions imposed upon him—five years elapsed from the birth of Joseph to the arrival of Jente. Withdrawing from the scholarly community and forgoing intellectual creativity was particularly difficult for him. One day Fromet helped him up to his study, where he shuddered at the sight of the clutter on his desk, the empty chair, and the bookshelves that Fromet had put to use for storing jars of jam. He felt like a dead man living, as if he was seeing his study in the state of neglect it would assume after his death.

Even during those bleak months when his spirits were at a particularly low ebb, when even the slightest effort caused him giddiness and he was almost unable to read, accept valued invitations, or follow events in the scholarly community, his public standing was unaffected. "I hope I will never be prevented from enjoying my life," Mendelssohn wrote to Michaelis in April 1771, a hope mingled with fear. About this time, the Jewish leaders of Berlin awarded him a special honor that gave the strongest proof possible of his status as the community's favorite son, appointing him an elder of the community. At a meeting on April 1, 1771, the community leaders decided that although Mendelssohn did not meet the formal requirements for the post of elder, and although it ran counter to the community's articles of association, "the articles are annulled for a great and important man such as he." His illness effectively made the appointment honorary at the time, but in the 1780s, after he had recovered and learned to live with his physical disabilities, he filled several senior posts in the Berlin community's executive institutions.

Several months later he also gained a royal honor when he was invited to Sanssouci Palace, the splendid summer residence of Friedrich II in Potsdam, not far from Berlin. The palace's architecture, its park, and its art treasures together constituted a consummate example of rococo culture. The palace, designed by the king himself, was intended to present the enlightened face of the Prussian kingdom and soften its rigid militaristic and bureaucratic image. The foreign minister of Saxony, Baron Thomas von Fritsch, was a guest at the castle and like the Crown Prince of Braunschweig wanted to meet the famed philosopher Mendelssohn. The king suggested that instead of von Fritsch traveling from Potsdam to Berlin, Mendelssohn should come to the castle. In the urgent official summons that reached Mendelssohn he was commanded to attend Sanssouci on Monday, September 30, 1771, at 11 A.M. The summons bore symbolic significance: the entry of the Jewish philosopher Mendelssohn

through the gates of the castle of King Friedrich II was perceived as a mark of the greatest esteem he could hope to attain.
News of the meeting was circulated in the correspondence of
the intellectual community. Mendelssohn's friends wanted to
know whether he had met the king face to face, and a drawing by Daniel Chodowiecki immortalized Mendelssohn's entry
through the gates of Potsdam—a diminutive Jew handing his
invitation to a tall Prussian soldier whose hat is removed in
admiration.

The invitation posed a dilemma for Mendelssohn, since the
meeting at the palace was to take place on the Eighth Day of
the Feast of Tabernacles. Emergency consultations were held
in the Berlin Jewish community, which were attended by the
community's rabbi, and it was decided that declining the king's
invitation was out of the question and that despite the sanctity
of the festival, Mendelssohn should travel to Potsdam by carriage, then enter the city on foot. The minister from Saxony
met with Mendelssohn face to face, but King Friedrich, who
that year had refused to approve Mendelssohn's election to the
Academy of Science, did not summon the most famous Jew in
his kingdom for a talk. Mendelssohn was reminded yet again of
a barrier in Prussia that could still not be surmounted by a Jew,
no matter how closely he might manage to approach it.

The two years between the Lavater affair and the visit to
Sanssouci were among the most difficult of Mendelssohn's life.
Those close to him followed his illness with great concern, and
many were convinced that it was a direct consequence of the
mental stress forced upon him by Lavater. It is more probable
that those pressures, over the course of more than a year, exacerbated the physical problems he had suffered since his forties.
The philosopher who took pleasure in speculative reflection in
his study on the second floor of his home, who composed a vast
number of critical treatises, who formulated brilliant proofs of

the soul's immortality, found himself having to fill a challenging and demanding role: to publicly represent generations of Judaism against Christianity on the stage of public opinion.

Mendelssohn had learned that the king, skeptical as he was in matters of religion, was not free of prejudices, was displeased with his success and fame, and was inclined to hinder his progress. Christian theologians also were concerned about his public status. Thus, for example, in a sermon he published in 1771, Johann Melchior Goeze, a Hamburg clergyman, warned of the danger to Christianity posed by the Mendelssohn phenomenon:

> He is, despite all his cleverness, a Jew, and his declarations sufficiently show how his mind is filled with thoughts against Jesus and his teachings. There is, therefore, in the exaggerated praise and compliments lavished upon him by Christians, scholars, and religious authorities, indisputable harm to the honor of our Savior, and they are inappropriate to the thoughts that true Christians should have regarding this man. They make the Jewish people, which is overly arrogant in any case, even more so and constitute a serious obstacle to its conversion.

Mendelssohn's public and personal hardships during those two years of affront and sickness reinforced his belief that the Enlightenment's main objective should be a stubborn effort to introduce the value of religious tolerance into the hearts of an ever greater number of his contemporaries.

6

━━━━━━◆❖◆━━━━━━

Dreams, Nightmares, and Struggles for Religious Tolerance

IN MID-1772 the values of the Enlightenment were tested within the Jewish sphere for the first time, when Mendelssohn came into conflict with a prominent representative of the rabbinical elite on the issue of the Jewish prohibition against delaying burial of the dead. The fear of death that Europeans experienced throughout the eighteenth century was complicated in the second half of that century by the findings of scientists. Physicians and researchers revealed that the cessation of breathing and pulse could no longer be accepted as a certain indication of death. They presented several horrific cases of people who had fainted, were thought to be dead, and were buried alive, after which neither their cries nor their knocking on the sealed coffin could be heard.

In the Duchy of Mecklenburg-Schwerin in northern Germany, Duke Friedrich implemented, by means of a special decree, the opinion of Professor Oluf Gerhard Tychsen that

Jewish burial customs mandating rapid burial of the dead frequently resulted in live burials. From a historical perspective, this measure had far-reaching implications: for the first time the state had brought to bear scientific research in order to intervene in the Jews' way of life and customs, demanding reforms and conformity with the values of the enlightened rulers, who strove for the welfare of all their subjects. The custom mandating the burial of a deceased Jew on the day of his death was perceived as life-threatening by Tychsen the scholar and Friedrich the ruler.

In the decree promulgated by the duke on April 30, 1772, the Jews of Mecklenburg-Schwerin were ordered to delay burying their dead for three days to make possible absolute confirmation of death. Because the decree mandated the discontinuation of an ancient religious custom, leaders of the duchy's Jewish community took measures to have it rescinded. In an urgent letter dispatched from Schwerin to Berlin, Mendelssohn's immediate intercession was requested. In this conflict between the enlightened state and the autonomous community, Mendelssohn was perceived as a negotiator who could capitalize on his fame, status, and familiarity with European culture to make the strongest possible case for the Jews' objections to the decree.

The letter, signed by the leaders of the Schwerin community, protested against what they perceived as a harsh edict aimed at "forcing the People of God to follow the laws of the Gentiles." Mendelssohn's assistance was sought on the assumption that he shared the traditional fundamental position of striving to maintain the way of life unique to Jews. Mendelssohn's response was ambivalent. At this stage of his life, having comprehended that both a Jewish and a Christian public was observing him and according him public leadership roles, he felt the weight of the responsibility placed upon him as the spokesman of the Jews of Germany. Consequently, he came to the aid of the Jews of the duchy and sent them a draft "petition" addressed to the duke, requesting that he amend his edict and accept a physician's approval for burial without waiting for three days to elapse. It is inconceivable, he wrote, that Jews would bury a person if there were any doubt whatsoever regarding his death. He implied that Duke Friedrich's unprecedented act not only questioned the wisdom and morality of Judaism but constituted a violation of the Jews' freedom to live in accordance with the laws of their religion, and consequently it was an act that violated religious tolerance. "As Jews," Mendelssohn wrote, "we are bound by the laws of our religion to fully accept the rulings of our rabbis, live in accordance with their commands, and direct all our actions in accordance with the rules and instructions of the religion."

After resolving the issue in the shared arena of the Jews and the state, Mendelssohn studied the debate in terms of internal Jewish discourse, as a conflict between Jewish leaders and modern medicine. Contrary to his recommendation to the duke, in his letter to the community leaders he recommended that the proposed amendment be incorporated into the burial customs. Mendelssohn derided the notion that the duke's act constituted a plot for religious conversion. Mendelssohn supported the scientists of his time and concurred with their opinion that in the first day, even two, unconsciousness might sometimes be mistaken for death. He enlisted his knowledge of Talmudic sources to establish his position on religious and historical arguments. He argued that saving lives takes precedence over the custom of immediate burial. He further proposed building a cave in cemeteries where the body would remain for three days in accordance with the ancient custom of cave burial in the Land of Israel. Thus, even if the duke rejected his proposal to allow burial in accordance with a pronouncement of death by a physician, cave interment would fulfill the terms of the duke's decree without violating religious custom. The concluding sentence of Mendelssohn's letter attests to his awareness that the proposal was problematic, and might even be seen as offensive and subversive by the rabbinical leadership: "I know, however, that you will not agree with me for the hand of custom is mighty and strong and it is possible that in your eyes I shall seem a heretic—but I have a clear conscience."

Within a few weeks Mendelssohn discovered that his proposals were indeed considered dangerously bold. He learned that, unbeknownst to him, the Schwerin community leaders had initially sought the religious opinion of Rabbi Jacob Emden of Altona, and that in their request to Mendelssohn, which was made with the rabbi's knowledge, they had concealed his absolute opposition to any change in burial customs. Mendelssohn was embarrassed when Rabbi Emden himself told him of this in a letter. He was forced to defend his position to a rabbi with whom he shared mutual respect but who regarded Enlightenment culture with suspicion. In the summer of 1772 they conducted, through an exchange of letters, a debate on their interpretations of the Talmudic sources on cave burial and the prohibition against delayed burial—a debate ostensibly religious but in fact ideological. Emden, who was known for his fiery spirit and zealous persecution of anyone who objected to his opinion, was shocked that Mendelssohn sided with science. Although he displayed great interest in the scientific innovations of his time, he believed that anyone giving first precedence to science was by definition positioning himself against religion, and there could be no possibility of compromise or agreement. Emden's positions were steadfast: it was inconceivable to question a custom of the forefathers throughout the Jewish Diaspora, it was unthinkable to offer a new proposal without the authoritative basis of one of the great rabbis, and the customs of the Gentiles must not be taken into consideration, for the Jews are commanded "to be separate from them and their laws." In his opinion, any consideration of scientific conclusions threatened the integrity of Jewish religious law: "Heaven forbid that we should pay attention to them in connection with the laws of the Torah, for then, Heaven forefend, its foundations will be weakened and its pillars will tremble . . . [for] there is no real substance in the words of a doctor that are devoid of Torah."

Mendelssohn's equally intractable insistence on his positions frustrated Rabbi Emden. He was surprised by Mendelssohn's refusal to accept his "truths" and rabbinical authority, and the proposal of reverting to cave burial appeared to him unrealistic, intolerable, and arrogant by its very innovation: "Who would not wonder and marvel at your arrogance in expressing such notions before me, to introduce from now on, to compel the people of Israel dispersed to the four corners [of the world] to make recesses [caves] the likes of which were never seen or imagined by our forefathers?"

Toward the end of his last letter in their debate, Emden gave Mendelssohn an unmistakable warning. He should know, Emden wrote, as one who walks the line between the culture of the Enlightenment and that of the Jews, that some question his orthodoxy and loyalty to Judaism. Emden entreated that Mendelssohn take his advice, "lest bitter and indignant men have cause to harm you when they hear that you are turning toward Gentile nonsense and seeking to change a custom of Israel the holy nation." Three years after Lavater had portrayed Mendelssohn as drawing closer to Christianity, a principal representative of the rabbinical elite informed him that adopting the new science and the values of the Enlightenment could call into question his affinity to Judaism and religious Jewish leaders. Mendelssohn's precise position on Jewish religion, which was not uncritical, was actually made explicit in his letter to Lavater some two years before the conflict with Emden:

I shall not deny that in my religion I have discerned additions and distortions made by Man which, alas, dull its splendor. What lover of truth can pride himself in that he found his entire religion pure of harmful man-made laws? We all seek the truth, we know the deleterious folly of hypocrisy and superstition, and hope we shall possess the ability to rid ourselves of it without damage to the true and the good. But I am truly convinced that the essence of my religion is immovable.

The issue of delayed burial simmered until the end of the century. The correspondence between Mendelssohn and Emden was publicized in the 1780s in order to provide support for Jewish modernists who advocated delayed burial. It was the most sensitive issue on the agenda during this period, a defining question in one of modernity's confrontations: between the traditionalists who opposed the Enlightenment and the innovators who tried to bring the values of the Enlightenment into Jewish society and culture. Mendelssohn was not alarmed by Emden's ominous warnings about the community's suspicions, and even continued to correspond with the renowned rabbi of Altona. In 1773, for example, he discussed with him another fundamental issue that had troubled him since the Lavater affair—the theological status of Righteous Gentiles who observe the Noahide Laws because they seem logical rather than out of adherence to divine laws. On this issue, too, which was central to Mendelssohn's tolerant worldview, he clashed with Rabbi Emden's uncompromising position. Mendelssohn leveled a philosophical and moral protest against the implications of Emden's insistence that only those who believe in the Law of Moses would attain salvation. "For me, words are as impenetrable as a hard rock," Mendelssohn wrote in response to Emden's declaration of the exclusivity of Judaism. "Should all the inhabitants of the earth except ourselves be doomed to perdition unless they believe in the Torah, which was given as an inheritance to the congregation of Jacob alone?" Mendelssohn, the Jewish human-ist and man of Enlightenment culture, could not conceive that God's grace is not universal and does not encompass all human beings: "What, then, shall the nations do who are not recipients of the light of the Torah? . . . Does God, then, treat his creatures in the way of a tyrant though they committed no injustice?"

Mendelssohn's health gradually improved in the summer of 1772, even as he conducted his confrontational correspondence with Rabbi Emden. Emden congratulated him in one of his letters: "My eyes lit up upon hearing that your health is restored, thank God, and my joy is increased for I have seen your strength then as it is now to converse in the war of the Torah." Mendelssohn resumed his routine work while convalescing for some months at the country home of one of the community's wealthy leaders, the silk manufacturer Eisik Dessau, in the Tiergarten woods on the banks of the River Spree. Dessau was the brother-in-law of the banker Daniel Itzig, and it seems that Mendelssohn, who had assured Fromet only ten years earlier that he would keep his distance from the affluent elite, was now a protégé of wealthy, influential, and well-connected Jews. In 1773, when on his physicians' advice he traveled to Bad Pyrmont, the renowned health spa for aristocrats, the hardships of the journey were alleviated by an invitation to ride in the comfortable carriage of Sacharia Veitel Ephraim, the son of Veitel Heine Ephraim, the community leader who had accumulated great wealth during the Seven Years' War. Bathing in the springs, taking the waters, and mingling with good company improved Mendelssohn's health and disposition, although on his return journey to Berlin he contracted a fever. He revisited the spa in the summer of 1774, this time traveling with Madame Rösel Meyer, Sacharia Veitel Ephraim's sister and wife of the banker Aaron Meyer Joresch. During his visit to Bad Pyrmont in July 1774, Mendelssohn was the focus of social interest for many vacationers from the German elite. He became friends with Count Wilhelm and Countess Marie Eleonore of the Duchy of Schamburg-Lippe, with whom he began to correspond. Rösel Meyer wrote in the margins of one of Mendelssohn's letters to Fromet: "I am compelled to tell you that you will be receiving to your home, God willing, a remarkably healthy husband. . . . Everyone here seeks his company and desires introduction to him, and he is especially enjoying the company of Graf and Grafin von Bückeburg."

Mendelssohn joined the pantheon of German dignitaries that year when two renowned minters from Berlin, Jakob Abraham and his son Abraham Abrahamson, produced a silver medal with his portrait in a series of coins commemorating great scholars. Mendelssohn's portrait appeared on one side of the coin, and on the other a human skull adorned with a butterfly, symbolizing his masterpiece, *Phädon*. He was also commemorated in a number of copper engravings and paintings during the 1770s and 1780s, as he attained the status of cultural icon. He continued to be beset by illness from time to time, but during periods of partial physical recovery he gradually resumed his intellectual and social activity—reading and keeping abreast of innovations in literature and philosophy, corresponding, writing essays, conducting philosophical debates, attending Berlin's theaters and receiving visitors. In addition to the two trips to Bad Pyrmont, he made several business trips, including visits to the Leipzig Fair, to Hanover, to Lessing again at the Wolfenbüttel library, to Dresden in the Electorate of Saxony and to his hometown Dessau (a journey on which he was accompanied by Fromet and David Friedländer, a maskil and wealthy merchant with whom he had recently become friends), to Memel and to Königsberg in eastern Prussia. On these trips he met intellectuals who were old friends and made the acquaintance of members of the aristocracy, high-ranking officials, and, of course, scholars. Some of them—for example, Adolph Friedrich August Hennings, the enlightened and energetic diplomat from the Kingdom of Denmark—with whom Mendelssohn became friends and close confidants, and with whom he corresponded frequently.

In the 1770s it became clear that the Schwerin community's request for his intercession with the duke on the issue of delayed burial had set a precedent. Mendelssohn's status and fame increasingly made him the advocate to whom Jewish communities came with their difficulties, and he accepted the role of the Jew defending his people in the name of the values of enlightenment, humanism, and the principle of religious tolerance. In 1775 representatives of the small Swiss communities requested his intercession in thwarting a decree limiting the number of Jews with residential rights. Mendelssohn swallowed his pride and sent an urgent letter to his one-time adversary, the Swiss clergyman Lavater—four years after severing all contact with him—requesting that he exert his influence. Mendelssohn admitted that he had no direct knowledge of the situation of the Jews in Switzerland, "but I can imagine their wretched existence considering the general attitude toward my nation, which virtually everywhere are regarded as strangers on God's earth, and from my knowledge of the particular situation in your country." And indeed, the "Friend of Humanity," as Mendelssohn called him, quickly acted on Mendelssohn's request, and the decree was soon rescinded.

Two years later the Jews of Dresden found themselves facing a similar problem: many of them faced expulsion, unable to pay the tax levied upon them for the right to reside in the city. "We appeal to you," wrote the community leader Samuel Halberstadt on behalf of his community, "that you may come to our aid, in support of your brethren, and that you may offer me your help, with God's mercy and your learned tongue, to find succor for my people, for when you see the remote dispersion of your brethren you will be unable to ignore it." Likening

Moses Mendelssohn to the biblical Moses, the Dresden Jews pinned their hopes of salvation on him: "We have put our trust in the Almighty that when Moses will raise his hand his right hand will aid us, and his strength will intercede on our behalf, and with his wisdom he will save and protect the city. . . . And peace and tranquility will return to Israel and there will be no fear." It was common knowledge that Mendelssohn was acquainted with the Saxon foreign minister, Baron von Fritsch, whom he had met at the royal palace in Potsdam six years earlier, and the community leaders suggested an appeal to the baron for assistance. Mendelssohn immediately responded to the letter, which he received during his visit to Hanover: he had been shocked, he wrote, to hear of the dire situation in Dresden—"My knees literally trembled with the dismay and apprehension that befell me"—and he had appealed to another senior official in the Saxony government for assistance, Friedrich Wilhelm Freiherr von Ferber.

When Mendelssohn had been required, during his visit to Dresden in the summer of 1776, to pay the notorious *leibzoll*, poll tax—a sum of twenty groschen imposed on the transit of cattle and Jews from place to place—von Ferber, counselor to the prince-elector of Saxony, considered the tax an affront to the famed philosopher, and interceded and obtained a special permit for Mendelssohn entitling him to visit the city without having to pay. Mendelssohn and the Saxon baron had become friends, and Mendelssohn appealed to him to ameliorate the situation of the Jewish community in Dresden. His indignation and his empathy with the Jews of Dresden were profound, as in every instance when he was confronted with the harsh reality of the life of Jews in Europe. "Expulsion is for a Jew the harshest punishment," he wrote to von Ferber; "more than mere banishment it is virtual extirpation from God's earth, for prejudice turns him away at every border with an iron fist." Was it conceivable, asked Mendelssohn, that human beings who are free of guilt and trespass should suffer this harshest of punishments simply because they adhere to different principles of belief? Mendelssohn concluded his highly emotional letter — "My heart is so heavy, my spirit is in turmoil, and I cannot compose myself" — by expressing the only hope in which he could find comfort: that fear of crimeless punishment would not prevail under a benevolent regime and a government of friends of humanity. Von Ferber was receptive to Mendelssohn's presentation of the discriminatory policy against the Jews as a test case for the application of the values of the Enlightenment, and, as with his petition on behalf of the Jews of Switzerland, the expulsion order threatening almost half the Jews of Dresden was rescinded.

Mendelssohn exploited his international standing one more time in the mid-1770s when he interceded at his own initiative to thwart one of the last blood libels against the Jews, proclaimed by the declining Kingdom of Poland. Two Jews in Warsaw had been accused of committing a religious murder, and a newspaper report on their imprisonment incensed Mendelssohn. Along with two of the Berlin Jewish community's leaders, he dispatched a letter of protest in French to one of the Polish aristocrats, who apparently maintained trade relations with Jews from Berlin, and demanded that the charges be dropped. We have no information about the result of his effort.

Mendelssohn's advocacy, dating to the 1750s, for universal application of the values of religious tolerance on behalf of oppressed Jewish communities was one of issues dearest to him. His longest journey outside Berlin in the 1770s—in the summer of 1777 to Königsberg, with David Friedländer and Benjamin Veitel Ephraim—incorporated an attempt to rescind another discriminatory decree that manifested Christian mistrust. According to the decree, prayers in the synagogue must be conducted under the supervision of a Christian official to ensure compliance with the order prohibiting articulation of the words, in the *Aleinu* prayer, "for they bow to vanity and emptiness," which were construed as anti-Christian. Even before departing for Königsberg, Mendelssohn composed a memorandum for the Christian community explaining that this prayer predated Christianity and consequently was neither directed against nor detrimental to it. During his visit he held a series of meetings with distinguished personages in an effort to end Christian supervision over prayers in the synagogue.

At one stage of his journey to Königsberg, after departing Polish territory, he shared his feelings about Poland's backwardness with Fromet: "It is a country where *Tisha B'Av* [a fast day] is a festival, and the only concern here is over superstition and brandy." By contrast, waiting for him in Königsberg was the philosopher Immanuel Kant. "Having a man of such gentle disposition, and good spirits and intelligence for a constant and intimate companion in Königsberg would be the kind of spiritual nourishment which is completely lacking here," Kant wrote to a former student, the physician Markus Herz, in Berlin soon after the visit. Kant considered Mendelssohn's visit to the university and attendance at two of his lectures a remarkable gesture. Many of the city's dignitaries sought Mendelssohn's company, and his departure was mentioned in the newspaper. For Mendelssohn it was like a royal visit that constituted proof of the powerful status he had acquired.

In the early spring of 1777 Mendelssohn wrote a personal letter to the innovative educator and director of the Philanthropin Educational Institute in Dessau, Joachim Campe, which attests to his dreams and aspirations at the time. Perhaps in spite of everything, he wrote, the culture of the Enlightenment would loosen the grip of prejudice against Jews and improve their civil status. He viewed Campe's willingness to accept Jewish students and appoint outstanding graduates to teaching positions as a step in the right direction. Only an institution that displays genuine religious tolerance, he noted, draws no distinction between those who are circumcised and those who are not. He considered it proof of a trend that supported a somewhat more optimistic view. The appointment of Jews to the Academy of Science (his own case), the acceptance of Jewish scholars into natural science societies (the medical practitioner from Berlin, Markus Bloch), and the appointment of Emanuel da Costa as secretary of the London Academy of Sciences encouraged him and gave him cause for cautious optimism. Even the memory of the proposal made in the seventeenth century to appoint Baruch Spinoza to the post of lecturer of philosophy at the University of Heidelberg survived as proof of the change taking place in European society with regard to the inclusion of Jews in the general community of scholars. This hopeful evidence, it seems, made him forget for a moment not only the fate of the Jews of Dresden, Switzerland, and Warsaw on whose behalf he had interceded, but also the frustrating fact that his election to the Royal Academy had not been approved by the king.

Soon, though, he was again beset by doubts about the Enlightenment's capacity to eradicate the prejudices and superstitions that prevented the attainment of civil and personal happiness by all human beings, and which had specifically suppressed generations of Jews. In the last decade of his life, Mendelssohn seems to have become increasingly sensitive to attitudes in Europe towards the Jews. His responses ranged from fervent excitement when he noted a significant increase in tolerance and humanism, to despondency and frustration when he realized how immensely difficult it was to bring about real change, to near-despair when contemplating the vast chasm between his personal status among the enlightened public and that of the Jews in general.

In 1778–1779 Mendelssohn's sensibilities received opposite signals. His close friend Lessing, who still served as librarian at Wolfenbüttel, had run afoul of the Christian establishment.

The philosopher Hermann Samuel Reimarus had died a decade earlier, leaving behind a long, handwritten theological treatise. Lessing took up the work and published it, in installments over a five-year period, as *Fragments by an Anonymous Writer*. The treatise leveled deistic criticism against Christianity, and the last *Fragment*, published in 1778, included a radical critique of the New Testament. When Lessing's role in the publication became known, a wave of accusations and condemnation rose against him. Church authorities issued a decree banning the *Fragments* and preventing Lessing from publishing any further theological essays.

Shortly afterward Lessing wrote the play *Nathan der Weise* with the aim of expressing indirectly, in a distant historical context—medieval Jerusalem during the Crusades—his mistrust of religious fanaticism. One of Lessing's characters decries "the pious rage to own the better god," harsh criticism against the perception of exclusivity and primacy of each of the three monotheistic religions, which would "on the whole world to force this better, as best of all." The shared destiny of all human beings, whoever they may be, takes precedence in Lessing's play over the differences between religions and histories. Religious fanaticism and religious discrimination are portrayed as immoral. Nathan the Jew relates a parable to the Muslim Sultan Saladin: each of the three religions, according to its own tradition, received a ring directly from God. It was impossible to discern which of them possessed the original, true ring and which possessed replicas of it. It was even possible that none of the three rings was the original. Consequently, further conflict and dispute are futile, and mutual recognition, coexistence, religious tolerance, and a state of religious pluralism are possible: "If each of you has had a ring presented by his Father, let each believe his own the real ring. 'Tis possible the father chose no longer to tolerate the one ring's tyranny." The metaphor was a special and personal gift from Lessing to Mendelssohn. Not only did the play identify with the harsh fate of the Jews persecuted, murdered, and humiliated by Christian fanatics, not only did it confront German public opinion with the struggle for religious tolerance in a most resolute way, but it also celebrated Mendelssohn himself in the character of Nathan the Wise. All who read or saw the play recognized the contemporary Berlin philosopher in the character of the paragon who displays wisdom, benevolence, tolerance, and love.

Mendelssohn was beside himself with joy and gratitude. For him this was a further indication that the Enlightenment's march of progress had not ground to a halt and that the values of tolerance had many advocates and impressive spokesmen like Lessing. In contrast with Voltaire's pessimistic criticism, as articulated in *Candide*—his treatise on the injustices of the world—Lessing succeeded, in Mendelssohn's view, in presenting a positive model of the Enlightenment based on Leibniz's optimistic view that all is for the best. The theatrical encounter in Crusader Jerusalem between a Jew, a Christian, and a Muslim created by Lessing ends in surprisingly familial harmony. The play portrays the benevolence of divine providence and conveys the message that the Divine Plan is for pluralism, for the coexistence of diverse ways of life and of religion.

As gratified as Mendelssohn was by his friend's enlightened advocacy of tolerance on behalf of Mendelssohn and the Jews, however, he soon suffered from the knowledge that Lessing was to pay a heavy personal price for his courage. Some Christian critics declared *Nathan der Weise* offensive to the religion. They drew parallels between the criticism leveled in the *Fragments* and the play: the Christian patriarch is presented as a villain, the persecution of Nathan and his family is described as an atrocity perpetrated in the name of religion, and the Jew is presented sympathetically as the true embodiment of "Christian" benevolence. "For is not Christianity all built on Judaism?" says the Friar in the play. "Oh, it has often vexed me, cost me tears, that Christians will forget so often that Our Savior was a Jew." Mendelssohn followed news of the hostile reactions against his friend with profound sadness. Only a little more than a year elapsed between the time the controversy over the play began in 1779 and Lessing's death in February 1781. For Lessing this was an extremely bitter period; he felt that his persecutors had triumphed over him and his friends had shunned him, leaving him isolated and depressed. Much to Mendelssohn's distress, the advocates of tolerance had been defeated by advocates of prejudice. When he heard of Lessing's death, Mendelssohn wrote: "He wrote *Nathan der Weise* and died. I cannot imagine any intellectual work surpassing *Nathan*, as far as *Nathan* in my eyes surpasses all that he had written before. He could not rise higher without arriving at a region beyond the reach of our mortal sight. . . . He was indeed more than a generation in advance of his century."

In the meantime, as he approached fifty years of age, the Berliner inspiration for Nathan the Wise continued his slow recovery from the illness that had restricted his activities for years. His home again became an open house for the inquisitive, for dignitaries and scholars from Prussia and beyond. His salon was filled with visitors on an almost daily basis, and animated discussions were common. Visitors on Friday evenings and Holy Days were for the most part relatives and Jewish friends, and the subjects discussed included the Torah Portion of the Week, Hebrew books, the state of the Hebrew language, the standard of Jewish education, and the fate of the Jews. Naturally, not all Berlin Jews admired Mendelssohn, and some criticized him behind his back. As Rabbi Jacob Emden had warned him, some questioned Mendelssohn's loyalty to Judaism. Hennings, one of his closest Christian friends, observed that he had heard "more than one wise Jew saying that Mendelssohn was given to fantasizing." Describing his sense of isolation as a philosopher in Jewish society, Mendelssohn wrote: "I have not a single friend from our people around me to truly participate with me on intellectual matters." Nevertheless, he gained considerable pleasure from the Friday evening and Holy Day gatherings. The host would sit in an armchair in the corner of the salon near the window and direct the conversation, introduce new visitors, praise and respond. When a debate became heated, he would rise from his armchair to try to reconcile opposing views.

In addition to her duties as wife and mother, Fromet bore most of the burden of hosting these salon gatherings. In 1775 the Mendelssohns suffered another calamity when their six-year-old son Mendel died. Their daughter Jente was born the same year and Abraham a year later. Their daughter Sise was born in 1778 but died just three months later. The parents devoted much attention to the children's education and upbringing. The family's status and financial means gave the children the advantage of studying with private tutors rather than at the community's *heder* and Talmud Torah school. The girls, Brendel and Reikel, concentrated on European languages and literature, while first and foremost in the boys' education was study of Torah and the acquisition of fluency in the Hebrew language. After Abraham's death, Mendelssohn devoted special effort to his son Joseph's education. When Joseph was six, Moses hired Solomon Dubno as a private tutor. Mendelssohn had come to respect Dubno, a scholar from Poland who was well versed in the Torah, the biblical commentaries, and the Hebrew language. Mendelssohn himself taught his son the Pentateuch, endeavoring to accommodate his son's linguistic skills by translating the ancient Hebrew text into German, in which all the Mendelssohns, as much of the Berlin Jewish community, were fluent. Dubno was engaged to methodically teach Joseph the rules of Hebrew grammar. Two years later another tutor was engaged—Herz Homberg, a young maskil from Bohemia who taught the children Hebrew and other subjects and soon became Mendelssohn's treasured confidant. The efforts invested in Joseph Mendelssohn's elementary education produced one of Mendelssohn's greatest works—his commentary of the Pentateuch, known as the *Bi'ur* (exegesis).

This became part of a German translation project undertaken in a renewed burst of creative energy. Mendelssohn, together with a team of maskilim and businessmen, produced over several years the new exegesis and a quality printing of the Pentateuch, *Sefer Netivot Hashalom* (The book of the paths of peace), which were published between 1780 and 1783. The initiative for the project, according to Mendelssohn, was Dubno's. In the extensive introduction to the *Bi'ur* Mendelssohn wrote:

> When God in His grace gave me sons and the time arrived to teach them Torah . . . I took it upon myself to translate the Torah into a decorous and refined German, such as that used in our time. I put the translations into their mouths when teaching them the text . . . so as to introduce them to the intent of Scripture, its idiomatic figures of speech, and the fine points of its reading.

The innovation of Mendelssohn's teaching method was immediately apparent to anyone who had been raised in the traditional education system of Ashkenazi Jewish society. Translation was, of course, inevitable when Hebrew was not a spoken language but the holy tongue, the language of culture and of the biblical texts. Consequently, teachers and young students alike in the heder and Talmud Torah schools became acquainted with the Torah through the mediation of Yiddish—the spoken language of Ashkenazi Jews. Mendelssohn believed that this teaching method was essentially flawed, that Yiddish, as a low hybrid language, was incapable of conveying the Bible's full aesthetic, ideological, and conceptual wealth that was embodied in the high Hebrew language. Although Yiddish served Mendelssohn in his everyday encounters with Jews, including his family, he contended that it contributed to Jewish alienation. In fact, he believed that Yiddish contributed "not a little to the immorality of the common man, and I look for excellent results from the recent increase among my brothers of the use of the pure German dialect."

Solomon Dubno, who when he came to tutor Joseph was the first to see Mendelssohn's German translation of the Torah as it was being rendered, encouraged him to incorporate a commentary and have it published. Mendelssohn was initially reluctant, agreeing only on the condition that his name not be mentioned, but he soon involved himself deeply in the project. What began in the private sphere—as an innovative method of teaching the Bible to his son Joseph by translating it into the language of the high culture in which Mendelssohn was deeply rooted—shifted to the public sphere and became a project that provoked many disputes and controversies.

The plan to publish the *Bi'ur* became public in 1778 when Solomon Dubno distributed in Amsterdam, the capital of Hebrew publishing, a number of sample pages with a prospectus entitled *Alim Litrufah* (Leaves for healing). The purpose was to secure advance subscriptions to fund the high publishing costs, estimated at 3,000 thalers. In a lengthy introduction Dubno presented Mendelssohn's translation both as a peak in the unbroken history of Bible translations into foreign languages and the answer to an urgent need of the time. He contended that the Hebrew language was being forgotten, existing translations were flawed, and reliance upon Christian translations into German left Jewish readers vulnerable to the translators' predisposition toward Christian theology and their disregard for the traditions of the Jewish Sages. Dubno presented Mendelssohn as a savior who in his benevolence and sensitivity to the tribulations of his Jewish brethren sought to contribute to the solution of the problem: "All this has been witnessed by the famed scholar our teacher Moses of Dessau, who has heard and understood, who has taken pity on his people, and translated the Five Books of Moses into very clear German language, a simple and lucid translation." The poet Naphtali Herz Wessely—one of the early maskilim and a colleague of Mendelssohn's who four years later published a plan for comprehensive reforms of the Jewish education system—added his personal recommendation to *Alim Litrufah,* as well as a florid and emotive song of praise (*Mehalel Re'a,* Praising a friend) that identifies the *Bi'ur* project as a historic turning point of incalculable importance. Wessely believed that the *Bi'ur* was the remedy for the severe deficiencies of Jewish education:

> Ignorance has become widespread among our people. . . . They send their children to school at the age of four or five, to teachers of Bible, without even taking note that they speak with a stammering tongue, and sometimes do not even know how to read properly. . . . [And one year later the teachers] will inform the parents: your children have already succeeded in learning Mishnah and Talmud, so it is no longer fit to teach them Bible. . . . Hence their words are bothersome to these lads, and press upon them like a heavy burden, and most of them, when they grow up, will cast the yoke of Talmud, and as they turn aside from it, nothing will remain with them, neither Torah nor the element of Jewish faith. . . . They do not even know how to read Hebrew and hence will not understand the words of the prayers they utter each day.

Mendelssohn's German translation, said Wessely, would improve proficiency in the Hebrew language, endear the Bible to the young students, improve the standard of the teachers, and address the acute Jewish identity crisis.

To what extent was Mendelssohn aware that the *Bi'ur* project, begun to educate his son, was being accorded such comprehensive significance? In a letter to Hennings, Men-

delssohn revealed that he had become involved in the enterprise because of the circumstances of his life and not by design.
However, what had begun as a practical solution to the lack of
an appropriate translation of the Torah from which to teach his
young children had become a vehicle for effecting a change in
direction in Jewish culture:

> In the original plan of my life, which I made in my better
> years, I was far from becoming an editor or translator of the
> Bible. I aspired to restrict myself to the business of the silk
> industry during the day and to my love of philosophy in my
> spare time. But Providence led me in a different direction. I
> lost the ability for philosophical reading, and as a result the
> principal part of my happiness. After some examination I
> found that the remains of my strength could still suffice to
> render a good service to my children and perhaps to a goodly
> portion of my nation if I were to put in their hands a better
> translation and explanation of the Holy Books than they pre-
> viously had. This is the first step to culture, from which my
> nation, alas! is kept at such a distance that one might well de-
> spair of ever improving.

In this private letter Mendelssohn presents the translation
project as an unavoidable solution for the philosopher, whose
illness had preempted his desire to develop a speculative study
that had so captivated him since he discovered it in Berlin in
the early 1750s. When he realized that he had the ability to produce and manage the project, however, he also came to recognize that it was an important enterprise for all Jews. He hoped
that by means of the *Bi'ur* it would be possible on the one hand
to break free from the flaws of the Yiddish translations and
open the gates to European culture, and on the other to curb
the gradual flow of young Jews who were being alienated from
Judaism by traditional education.

The connection made both by Wessely and by Mendelssohn himself between the *Bi'ur* and the need to address the flaws in traditional education and to facilitate the development of Jewish culture turned the translation into a Jewish Enlightenment project—which in turn provoked the apprehension of several prominent rabbis. The more the *Bi'ur* was presented as a focus of elementary Jewish education, the more these rabbis feared that study of the Bible would jeopardize the Talmud's position of primacy.

Dubno and Mendelssohn presented the German translation as part of a continuing tradition of translation in Jewish culture down the generations and the *Bi'ur* as a compilation of classical commentaries, rather than groundbreaking or critical ones. Furthermore, they declared their intention to distance themselves from the new criticism leveled against the Bible and the Christian commentaries and translations. Still, the voices of the project's detractors were heard as soon as *Alim Litrufah* was published. Rumors reached Mendelssohn that Rabbi Ezekiel Landau of the Prague community and Rabbi Raphael Kohen of the Altona-Hamburg community were threatening to ban the *Bi'ur* even before the first book of the Pentateuch was published. One Hamburg newspaper even reported that Rabbi Kohen had already issued an excommunication order against anyone who read this Pentateuch. Although no such order was actually issued, Mendelssohn was troubled by the reactions, which he attributed to the rabbis' unwarranted religious fanaticism. At that point, in 1779, he saw himself as an innocent victim who was being persecuted for his literary activities. The sensitivity that had long tracked fluctuations in attitudes toward the Jews now began to track what was happening within Jewish society as well. Rabbi Landau, whom many regarded as the foremost rabbinical authority of eighteenth-century European Jewry, was suspicious of the project because the *Bi'ur* lacked a seal of rabbinical approval and because he feared that its primary purpose would be to learn German by means of the Bible.

Landau believed that presenting the Pentateuch with Mendelssohn's German translation required too much effort on the part of the teacher: "Now since the children will find it hard to understand it, the teacher will have to spend most of the time explaining German grammar, and consequently the young student will remain devoid of the elements of the Torah."

In a letter to Avigdor Levi, his friend from Prague, in the spring of 1779, Mendelssohn responded to the accusation that he had not approached Rabbi Landau with a request for approval. The custom of approbation had allowed the rabbinical elite to supervise printed publications in the sphere of Jewish culture. The project, Mendelssohn contended, did not require rabbinical supervision because it was not rabbinical literature. It was a textbook, written in German, and as such should come under a separate category exempt from rabbinical supervision. In fact, Dubno was in possession of three rabbinical approbations, the most important being an enthusiastic endorsement by Rabbi Zvi Hirsch Levin of Berlin, the community rabbi and a close friend of Mendelssohn's. Only a year earlier Rabbi Levin and Mendelssohn had cowritten, at the request of the Prussian authorities, a compilation of Jewish religious laws pertaining to personal status and property. It was no accident, then, that the approbations were not printed in *Alim Litrufah*—Mendelssohn printed them only when the project was completed in 1783. His intention was to draw a clear boundary between the rabbinical elite's sphere of authority and the literary project of the Jewish maskilim. Thus the *Bi'ur* became a Jewish Enlightenment project of far-reaching significance, as a manifestation of the emergence and growth of a new breed of elite Jewish scholars and philosophers—the elite of maskilim.

In any event, although the threats of banning angered him, Mendelssohn preferred to avoid a confrontation with these rabbis. He asked his friend Hennings, who dubbed the rabbis' reaction "theological despotism," only that he try to interest senior officials in the Kingdom of Denmark in the project. Mendelssohn's lifelong avoidance—typical of the German Enlightenment—of the radical criticism of the Christian Church and clergy common to intellectuals in Europe, especially France, gave him standing to make such a request. "As for me," he wrote, "I have no intention of either challenging or ridiculing them. After all, what would it profit me to put the scholars of my nation up to ridicule?" Hennings indeed managed to obtain subscriptions from the Danish monarch and the crown prince, which contributed to the prestige of the project and accorded it a measure of immunity against efforts to ban it. In a further letter to Hennings, which he wrote during his visit to Strelitz at the end of June 1779, Mendelssohn summed up, with a kind of philosophical equanimity, his feelings about this encounter with rabbinical fanaticism, the threats of a ban, and the aspersions cast on his loyalty to the Jewish religion:

> As a matter of fact, the ferment over my unfortunate book has not troubled me in the slightest. No fanatic is easily capable of making my cool blood boil, . . . my heart displays no signs of anger, concern, regret and so forth. . . . In the meantime the rabbi of Altona [Raphael Kohen] is keeping his thunder hidden. I do not know his intentions. He is perhaps waiting to strike . . . until the completed book is put before him. Let him do so! I wish that he be left undisturbed and that nothing be brought to bear upon him from the outside, in order to see what truth alone, free of all other considerations, is able to accomplish in my nation.

For all his lack of overt passion, however, a personal comment in his letter to Hennings reveals the extent to which he these threats had hurt him, and even betrays a degree of belligerence: "The more opposition this weak attempt [to march my people toward culture] meets, the more necessary it seems to me and the more zealously I shall seek to carry it through."

This was the second time, after his clash with Rabbi Emden in 1772 on the issue of delayed burial, that Mendelssohn had put the rabbinical elite of his time to the test of the Enlightenment.

The resistance of the rabbis did not succeed in putting a stop to the *Bi'ur* project. The costly and prestigious edition was completed in 1783, and added to the Jewish library were the Five Books of the Pentateuch, with a translation into German and a new and interesting commentary. The commentary was jointly written by Mendelssohn, Dubno, Wessely, Homberg, and Aaron Friedenthal, another tutor from Galicia. Mendelssohn supervised the work, dividing the commentaries on the Five Books between these maskilim, and with the help of David Friedländer he obtained a printing budget—by securing more than five hundred advance subscriptions from dozens of communities in Germany, Austria, Poland, Lithuania, and western Europe, who together paid for 750 copies of the *Bi'ur.* Mendelssohn appointed his brother Saul to be responsible for the accounts and to supply the books to the purchasers, in which he was aided by Jeremiah Bendix, his friend from Berlin's wealthy elite. He also addressed the crisis that arose when Dubno, frustrated that his philological skills were being insufficiently valued, abandoned the project at its peak.

As spring 1783 approached, and the printing of the Pentateuch was nearing completion, Mendelssohn wrote a long and scholarly preface (*Or La-Netivah,* Light for the path) in which he reviewed previously published translations of the Bible into foreign languages, explained the approach to the accompanying biblical commentaries (emphasis on the literal and linguistic meaning of the verses), and addressed the importance of the project. In particular Mendelssohn felt a need, probably in light of the suspicions raised against him, to emphasize his devotion and dedication to the fundamental principles of Jewish tradition. Thus, for example, he declared that wherever there was an apparent contradiction between what the commentators regarded as the literal meaning and the interpretation of the Sages, tradition had prevailed:

> If the approach which seems to us to be the *peshuto shel mikra* [literal or plain meaning] contradicts and opposes the received *derash* [interpretation] which is transmitted to us by our Sages, such that it is impossible that both can be correct, for the contradictory is precluded, then it is incumbent on us to go in the way of *derash*, and to translate the text according to it, because we have only the traditions of our Sages and in their instruction we see the light.

No less important was his declaration that his translation of the Pentateuch and the accompanying commentary were different from the New Testament in essence, because the Bible was perceived not merely as a book of sacred history but as a book of God's laws given to the Jews on Mount Sinai:

> Christian translators—who do not have the traditions of our Sages . . . for who will compel them to be beholden to that which they have not received from their forefathers . . . they will not accept the words of the Torah, or observe and do all that is written in it, but rather [consider it] a history book, to learn of events in ancient times and understand the ways of Providence and supreme leadership through the generations.

For him, Jewish study of the Bible was fundamentally different, for it embodied the essence of Judaism—God's laws which Jews are commanded to observe and practice. Treating it merely as history "may be acceptable to learned Christians and their students; for us Jews, this is unacceptable because for us this Torah is a legacy. . . . Knowing the commandments that God commanded us to study and teach, to preserve and observe, and it is our life and endurance." In 1778, when the *Bi'ur* project was at the stage of fund-raising for advance subscriptions, a further step was made in Berlin "toward culture" with the establishment of a modern Jewish school in the Ashkenazi tradition. Mendelssohn was not involved in this initiative, which was backed by the wealthy families of the Berlin community. As they increasingly assimilated to the Prussian state's civil and economic demand for functional and productive citizens with the skills, industriousness, and moral way of life to contribute to its strength, Jewish leaders felt increasingly responsible for cultivating the weaker groups in their society. Two of them, brothers-in-law Isaac Daniel Itzig and David Friedländer, undertook at their own philanthropic initiative to establish and run a *Freischule*, a school without tuition fees, for the children of poor families to supplement their daily Torah studies. In the afternoons at the Freischule they studied—under professional teachers and with German textbooks—mathematics, sciences, geography, and ethics. To fund the school Itzig and Friedländer founded the *Hevrat Hinukh Ne'arim* (Society for youth education) and raised large donations from the community's wealthy families. Once the school was established, the curriculum expanded to include Bible studies, Hebrew, and French. The new school gave children from the lower classes the opportunity to climb the socioeconomic ladder and participate in the economic activities of the Jewish capitalists as clerks or salesmen. The founders of the school petitioned King Friedrich II, presenting their objectives and declaring the ambition to help "make the Jews civilized and to educate them to become useful citizens of the state."

As soon as the *Bi'ur* was published, it became one of the school's textbooks. To aid the study of the German language, Friedländer published the *Lesebuch für jüdische Kinder* (Reader for Jewish children) in 1779. Friedländer was a young, enthusiastic maskil of twenty-eight from a family of Königsberg merchants; he had married one of the wealthy Itzig family's daughters. At about this time he and Mendelssohn became close friends and made their trips together to Dresden, Dessau, and Königsberg. Friedländer took it upon himself to raise funds for the printing of the *Bi'ur*, and made fruitful use of his family and business connections with wealthy Jews in Prussia's cities and elsewhere. Mendelssohn commended him when he published the list of subscribers: "I am grateful first and foremost to my ally and friend who is like a brother to me, the honorable David Friedländer, for he is my foremost helper and supporter."

The Hinukh Ne'arim School was the first modern educational institution in the Ashkenazi Jewish society, and the *Reader for Jewish Children* was the first modern textbook. Although Mendelssohn did not initiate this activity in the sphere of Jewish education, Friedländer incorporated in the German *Reader* texts written by Mendelssohn, including translations of several moral parables from the Talmud and a German translation of Maimonides' Thirteen Principles of Faith. Mendelssohn also wrote especially for the *Reader* a universal prayer entitled "Devotional Exercise of a Philosopher." In this prayer, which includes, among other sentiments, the supplication, "Let us be wise that we may be happy," Mendelssohn articulated his belief in humanism and in a natural religion whose values and principles are evident to all intelligent and moral human beings. Translations of the *Shema Yisrael* (Hear, O Israel) prayer, Maimonides' Thirteen Principles of Faith, and the Ten Commandments all represented the distinctiveness of the Jewish faith and expressed the commitment to observing the Torah and its commandments, but the philosophical prayer emphasized what all religions share, and it makes explicit Mendelssohn's approach: that God is the source of good, truth, wisdom, and love; that he creates nature and ensures harmony in the world by guiding human beings on the path to happiness. Printed on the cover of the *Reader for Jewish Children* was the emblem of Hevrat Hinukh Ne'arim—a medal adorned with flowers bearing the name of the school in Hebrew and German and beneath it an assortment of study material: books, notebooks, writing and measuring implements. The curriculum, the objectives, the specialized textbook, and the very name of the institution—Hinukh Ne'arim—attested to its founders' ambition to make it an alternative and a supplement to the traditional education of the Talmud Torah. The school incorporated Jewish Enlightenment dissatisfaction with traditional education methods and the intention to radically change the focus in Jewish schools from the holy content of the Torah to practical training and education.

By the end of the eighteenth century, suitable education for Jews, which had been a major topic of discussion in Mendelssohn's salon gatherings, became a key element in the debate throughout Europe on the place of the Jews in the modern state. Two events in 1781 provoked strong public reactions and compelled Mendelssohn's further reassessment of the rapid changes in the Jewish community's relation to the state. The first was the promulgation of a far-reaching plan that constituted a kind of package deal: radical improvement in the status of Prussian Jews in exchange for radical reform of their educational and commercial spheres. The plan, which was publicized in a tract entitled *Über die bürgerliche Verbesserun der Juden* (Concerning the amelioration of the civil status of the Jews), was initiated by the senior government official Christian Wilhelm von Dohm, a Christian scholar with an academic background and a member of Berlin Enlightenment circles. The plan, which was bold for its time, had begun with a petition from communities that were suffering hardship and whose leaders sought Mendelssohn's intercession. In the wake of a wave of anti-Jewish incitement that threatened the Jewish communities of Alsace in France, Cerf Berr, one of the Jewish leaders there, asked Mendelssohn to provide them an updated statement of defense. Mendelssohn forwarded the request to Dohm, presuming that a memorandum in favor of the Jews would carry substantially greater weight if written by a Christian scholar.

Dohm not only agreed to write the memorandum, he also devoted considerable thought to the issue of the Jews and the state of the Enlightenment in Europe. The result was a more comprehensive tract in which he analyzed the reasons for discrimination against the Jews and for their marginalization, refuted most of the customary accusations against them, and outlined a plan to rehabilitate them by means of improved education and retraining for productive occupations. His conclusion was sweeping: a state seeking to adopt the humanistic principles of the Enlightenment could not treat the Jews with the same barbarity that had characterized the era when religious fanaticism dictated government policy. The state had to acknowledge that the characteristics of the Jews in that earlier era that had rendered them incapable of making any real contribution to the state—the dubious morality of traders, overconcentration in trade, deficiencies in general education, and physical weakness—were the unfortunate consequences of age-old policies of discrimination. Those policies could not be continued. "The Jew is more a man than a Jew," declared Dohm in a tolerant spirit reminiscent of Lessing, hence the different customs of his religion did not constitute grounds for his exclusion from human and civil rights.

A few months later, at the beginning of October 1781—while an animated public debate was taking place on the question of whether Dohm's radical and surprising plan was feasible—the emperor of the Austrian Empire, Joseph II, issued the first in a series of Edicts of Tolerance for the Jewish communities under his rule. In changing the status of the Jews, the energetic emperor displayed remarkable sensitivity toward the status of the various minorities in the empire, an intent to foster the culture of Enlightenment, and an aspiration to improve efficiency in the state by establishing uniform rules for the entire population and stricter supervision by the bureaucratic system. Although these edicts fell well short of guaranteeing equal rights—in many places the restrictions on residence and occupation remained unchanged—this unprecedented institutionalization of the principle of religious tolerance was received enthusiastically in the Enlightenment camp. For the first time an absolutist but enlightened monarch had rescinded restrictions and discriminations that the Christian state had imposed upon its Jewish minority, and had at the same time offered Jews integration into the state by subordinating the communities to the state's bureaucratic system and by educating the younger generation in a school system centered around the German language and study of the sciences.

In the early 1780s Dohm and Joseph II seemed to have almost simultaneously opened new horizons for Jewish existence in the modern era. Both propositions offered far-reaching changes in customary patterns of existence—in the community's autonomy, educational institutions, relation to government authorities, economics (both Dohm and Joseph II recommended that Jews shift from trade to crafts and farming), and even in language and family. Mendelssohn responded to this sudden development in early 1782, in one of his most important and interesting treatises on the "Jewish question"—the Preface to Manasseh Ben Israel's *Vindiciae Judaeorum*, Vindication of the Jews. This treatise started a chain reaction that hurled Mendelssohn into new maelstroms.

In the 1650s the Portuguese Rabbi Ben Israel, who was one of the leaders of the seventeenth-century Amsterdam community, had visited London, where he waged a lone battle with the aim of obtaining England's consent to the return of the Jews. His lobbying activities with government officials during Oliver Cromwell's rule provoked ferment and opposition. This was one of the first rounds in the public debate on Jews at the start of the new era. In 1656 Ben Israel drafted in English and published in London *Vindiciae Judaeorum*, a short treatise refuting the arguments against readmission of Jews to England, from which they had been banished in 1290. Ben Israel devoted special attention to the brutality of the Catholic Inquisition and to the blood libels, as well as related allegations of a Jewish custom of cursing Christians in their prayers and cheating them in trade. Ben Israel contended that an impartial and unprejudiced reexamination of these false allegations would result in support for granting the Jews refuge in England. Since the dispersal of Jews to all the ends of the earth—"I conceived," wrote Ben Israel, "that by the *end of the earth* might be understood this *island*"—was a prerequisite for the redemption of Israel, their readmission to England would also, he wrote, hasten the coming of the Messiah. Mendelssohn was far from advocating a messianic vision such as the one that drove the seventeenth-century rabbi from Amsterdam, but when he sought to make his own contribution more than a century later to the renewed debate in Europe on the "Jewish question," he decided to publish a German translation of that same apologia on Judaism and Jews. In *Vindiciae Judaeorum* Ben Israel addressed numerous contentions made by Christians against Jews. In Mendelssohn's view this was a fine example of a successful struggle for rights for the Jews.

"At the present juncture, when so much is said and written both for and against the Jews," Mendelssohn wrote, "the Rabbi's tract appears to me well worth translating." It appears that Mendelssohn felt—especially after reading the modern apologia written by Dohm in Berlin as well as the first critical reactions to it—that his situation resembled that of Ben Israel in London and that perhaps he was playing a similar role as spokesman for the Jews. *Vindiciae Judaeorum*, Mendelssohn stressed, had been written at a time when Ben Israel had almost despaired of achieving his objective. The Preface reflects Mendelssohn's ambivalence as well as his agitation. In some places in the Preface he celebrated the indefatigable efforts of the rabbi that persuaded England to open its gates to the Jews—a victory for the principle of tolerance—but elsewhere he articulated his dejected conviction that a wall would forever block the way of tolerance: "It is curious to observe how prejudice assumes the forms of all ages, on purpose to oppress us, and puts obstacles in the way of our civil admission." His loftiest dreams and darkest nightmares were interwoven into the Preface he wrote at the end of the winter of 1781–1782.

At first Mendelssohn allowed himself to be swept up in the rising excitement over the new developments in the public debate concerning the Jews, to dream that the heavens were now opening and the aspirations of the enlightened humanists, pursuers of peace and tolerance, were finally being fulfilled. About four years before his death, Mendelssohn opened the Preface with the words: "Thank kind Providence, that I live to see yet, in my old days, the happy period, when the Rights of Man are beginning to be taken to heart, in their true extent." The publication of Lessing's play *Nathan der Weise*, Dohm's proposal to grant citizenship to Jews, and the Edicts of Tolerance promulgated by Emperor Joseph II had together created, in Mendelssohn's view, a new reality. He believed that the desire of Providence for peace on earth and man's vocation to exercise his natural rights to tolerance and liberty were being manifested by the emperor in a practical and applicable political approach. Mendelssohn clarified his historical position in an intriguing autobiographical note, modestly proclaiming his own lack of political aptitude and his consequent inactive role of philosopher in this drama, observing from without and dreaming of his wishes coming true. This was the statement of a loyal Prussian Jew living in Berlin under the rule of Friedrich II, a disclaimer of any intention to fan the flames so that other countries, including even Prussia itself, might follow the Austrian emperor's example:

I am at too great a distance from the closets of the great and whatever has any influence there, to be able to take any part, or cooperate in that great work. I live in a country, in which one of the wisest sovereigns that ever ruled over men made the arts and sciences flourish, and rational liberty of thinking become so universal, that the effects thereof extend to the humblest inhabitant of his realm. Under his scepter, I met with opportunity and inducement to cultivate my mind, meditate on my own destination, as well as on that of my brethren, and inquire, as far as I was able, into man, destiny, and Providence. But from the great, generally, and from any commerce with them, I have always been far removed. I all along lived retired, and felt neither inclined, nor called upon, to intermeddle with the affairs of the active world. . . . At that obscure distance, I still stand, awaiting with dutiful patience, what it may please an all-wise and all-kind Providence, to let result from this.

Clearly, Mendelssohn's self-attestation contains a deliberate diminishment of his status in the public arena. Nothing could have been further from the truth than that Mendelssohn, during the last twenty years of his life, had "all along lived retired." This modesty may have reflected the heartfelt desire of the philosopher who had been drawn into the role of spokesman of the Jews and was thus perceived both in general and Jewish public opinion, but it almost certainly also was meant as an obsequious reiteration of loyalty to the Prussian king and a politic deflection of suspicion that he might be encroaching on the highly sensitive political sphere in Prussia and joining forces with radical elements that were proclaiming equality and demanding greater liberty.

The Preface was first and foremost Mendelssohn's response to Dohm's immensely challenging tract. Although Mendelssohn himself had encouraged Dohm to write *Concerning the Amelioration of the Civil Status of the Jews*, and although he shared

Dohm's objective of persuading the eighteenth-century European state to expedite the granting of citizenship to the Jews, he thought Dohm's plan problematic, fundamentally flawed, possibly even dangerous. He initially lauded the Christian scholar as a voice of the Enlightenment. It was fortunate, Mendelssohn wrote, to have Dohm equating the rights of the Jews with the rights of mankind: "The philosopher of the eighteenth century takes no notice of difference of [religious] dogmas and opinions, he beholds in man *man* only." From that conciliatory opening, however, Mendelssohn undertook a bitter and intense dispute with Dohm's premise that the Jews needed fundamental regeneration and rehabilitation before they could be worthy of rights. Mendelssohn suspected that underlying Dohm's premise were the same tired prejudices as held by those who opposed Jewish citizenship. Mendelssohn was aghast at Dohm's account of the innumerable flaws in the Jews' way of life, economy, education, and morality. He felt much the same when, immediately afterward, he read the theologian Johann David Michaelis's critique of Dohm's plan. Standing in the way of Jewish citizenship, Michaelis wrote, were their self-identification as a separate nation, their messianic expectation of the return to Zion, and their religious laws that restricted military service and contact with non-Jews. Michaelis, who consistently expressed doubts regarding the possible integration of Jews into the general citizenship of the state, may have doubted that Jews could be loyal and skilled soldiers in the modern state, but Dohm himself rejected them from civil service, and both presented Jews as having a propensity for deceit and lawbreaking. In the Preface, Mendelssohn revealed—more explicitly than anywhere else in his published writings thus far—his dread of the Christian world and his doubts concerning the feasibility of the longed-for, fundamental change in Jewish-Christian relations. Could the Enlightenment, he asked, ever eradicate the traces of fanaticism and barbarism from Christian attitudes toward the Jews?

A comparison of the horrendous libels against Jews by Christian fanatics, as described by Ben Israel in an earlier, less-enlightened era, with the accusations still current revealed a shift, according to Mendelssohn: in the past the slanderers sought to transform Jews into fellow Christians, and now into useful citizens. But this was cold comfort, for Jews still serve no less as targets for insult and abuse:

> Formerly, all imaginable pains were taken with us, and several establishments provided for the purpose of making of us not useful citizens but Christians, and our being so very obstinate and stiff-necked, as not to let ourselves be converted, was held a sufficient reason to pronounce us a useless burden on society, and to invent, of such reprobate monsters, every possible horror and infamy, which might subject us to the contempt and abhorrence of the rest of mankind.

Now Jews were being accused, Mendelssohn added, of being unfit for citizenship: "Now it is even superstition and ineptitude; want of moral feelings, taste, and good manners; unfitness for the arts, sciences, and useful trades." Yet, he continued, the restrictions imposed upon Jews and their exclusion from full participation in the state prevent their development. Anyone who truly and honestly seeks the integration of Jews into society and culture, he wrote, must first release them from these restrictions, otherwise the oppression will continue forever: "We are still kept far removed from arts, sciences, useful trades, and the professions of mankind; every avenue to improvement is still blocked up to us, and the want of refinement made a pretence for our oppression. They tie our hands, and scold us for not making use of them."

On the question of whether Christian religious fanaticism had declined, Mendelssohn was extremely skeptical. He contended that the false legends attributed to the Jews had yet to be eradicated, and that on this matter the import of Ben Israel's apologia endured, more than a hundred years later. In a renewed burst of pessimism Mendelssohn informed his readers of the regrettable facts of life: the Enlightenment of the eighteenth century had not "trodden down all the tracks of barbarism in history." In many cities throughout Germany, a Jew still was not "suffered to go about in broad-day without a soldier by his side, for fear he should decoy a Christian child, or poison a well. At night, though ever so strictly guarded, he is not trusted at all within its walls, on account of his known commerce with evil spirits." Many Christians still took as the absolute truth one of the most trenchant anti-Jewish myths, which had arisen in the sixteenth-century Duchy of Brandenburg (which became the Prussian monarchy in 1701). In 1573 the Jews of Berlin and the entire duchy had been banished after Lippold, the minter and court valet, was convicted of murdering by poison Prince Joachim II and was brutally executed. Mendelssohn showed, however, that historians had uncovered documentary evidence that Lippold had no connection whatsoever with the prince's death, and that the confession wrung from him by atrocious torture had been false. His was a terrible fate. Mendelssohn vividly describes the tortures Lippold suffered after his interrogation:

> He was torn with red-hot pincers, in ten different parts of the town; then broken on the wheel, by a blow on each leg and arm. His body was quartered, and his entrails burned, along with the magic book, on a stage built for that purpose in the new market at Berlin. A more than ordinary great mouse, which came running forth from underneath the stage, and which no one could take for anything else but the demon of sorcery, delivered the spectators from all remaining doubt that the delinquent had been condignly dealt with.

The expulsion of the Jews of Berlin and Brandenburg therefore had been the outcome of a callous and unfounded libel,
the product of prejudice and superstition, but in Mendelssohn's
view the myth remained etched in the collective memory of the
Germans. Mendelssohn presented further evidence that not
"even in our enlightened times does that enlightenment extend
so far yet as to render those grosser charges quite innocuous."
He was referring to the blood libel that had occurred in the
Posen community in the 1730s: two of the community's rabbis
had been accused of murdering a Christian child and using his
blood for the celebration of Passover, and were severely tortured. "I shall spare the humane feelings of my readers," Mendelssohn wrote, "the details of these tortures: they were the
most horrible that barbarity ever indulged itself in."

Could this state of affairs be remedied? Mendelssohn asked,
could those "malicious calumnies," those "barbarous laws," and
that entire dark, onerous, oppressive Christian heritage dating
back to medieval times be successfully eradicated? At this point
in his life, Mendelssohn's despair deepened. Even if one could
cut through all the roots of an antiquated prejudice against
Jews, he feared, yet it could suck nourishment out of the air. A
mind so biased by prejudice would not pay attention to reason.
The struggle of the Enlightenment against hardheartedness
was then perhaps futile and hopeless: "Reason and Humanity
raise their voices in vain; for hoary Prejudice has completely
lost its hearing."

But even as Mendelssohn expressed these seemingly de-
spairing words, which could justifiably be construed as an admission of defeat and withdrawal from the struggle for religious tolerance, he clung to his dream. Against the measures
that Dohm proposed the state take in order to rehabilitate
and regenerate Jewish society so that its members could become useful and respectable citizens, Mendelssohn presented
an alternative model for the naturalization of the Jews. Being

a Jewish merchant and manager in the textile industry, he was personally offended by Dohm's assertion that the Jews are superfluous to the state when they engage in trade and not production. Mendelssohn proposed an economic model without state management, one based on free competition, freedom of occupational choice, and a dynamic market undisturbed by outside intervention. The contribution of Jewish merchants to the state, Mendelssohn declared, is enormous: "A merchant, while quietly engaged at his desk in forming commercial speculations, or pondering, while lolling on his sofa, on distant adventures, produces, in the main, more than the most active and noisy mechanic or tradesman." Without the merchant who moves and transports goods from one country to another, the entire economy would grind to a standstill. In this respect even the Jewish peddler is useful: "The pettiest trafficking Jew is not a mere consumer, but a useful inhabitant [*Einwohner*] (citizen [*Bürger*], I must not say), of the state—a real producer." In his view the state should not interfere in demographic processes. Mendelssohn denounced Dohm's fears—which were similar to those of the Prussian rulers—that the state would be inundated with "men superfluous to the state, men of whom a country can make no use at all." He protested discrimination against the weaker members of society: "No country can, without serious injury to itself, dispense with the humblest, the seemingly most useless of its inhabitants, and to a wise government, not even a pauper is one too many—not even a cripple altogether useless." Mendelssohn vehemently objected to state supervision of population migration and residence permits, which was particularly strict in Prussia and severely constrained the Jews. On this issue, too, he presented a liberal position, demanding that the state refrain from interference and supervision. He argued that natural laws of supply and demand apply to population migration as well as to economic activity: "There is no arrangement to oppose the accumulation of souls, no measure to put a stop to increase, that does not tend far more to injure the improvement of the inhabitants, the destination of man and his happiness, than is done by the apprehended overfilling. In this, let them depend upon the wise ordering of nature. Let it quietly take its course." According to Mendelssohn's vision, the Jews should be accepted as they are without placing impediments on them to change their way of life as a precondition for their acceptance. In his view, the ideal, liberal, and most humane naturalization should be implemented according to the precedent of Holland in the time of Ben Israel, with its underlying condition of assurance of liberty without custodianship, without supervision, without regulation, and without the imposition of preconditions and demands for rehabilitation and regeneration:

> What else but liberty, mild government, equitable laws, and the hospitable manner in which men of all complexions, garbs, opinions, manners, customs and creeds, are admitted, protected, and quietly allowed to follow their business? Nothing else but these advantages have produced, in Holland, the almost superabundant blessings and exuberance of prosperity, for which that country is so much envied.

In Mendelssohn's liberal dream the civil rights of the Jews would be successfully implemented when the modern centralist state adopted the pluralistic approach, relinquished its insistence on uniformity, and, in particular, withdrew its blatant interference in their lives—interference that paradoxically, according to Dohm, "the philosopher of the eighteenth century," should be deepened.

Mendelssohn complained that Michaelis had distinguished not between "Christians" and "Jews" but between "Germans" and "Jews," excluding Jews from the body of citizens. Deeply offended, Mendelssohn wrote: "He does not content himself with establishing the religious differences between us; he prefers to see us as strangers. . . . For how long, for how many millennia, must this distinction between the master of the land and the stranger continue? Would it not be better for mankind and culture to obliterate this distinction?" The state, Mendelssohn argued, should take the first step toward granting citizenship by ending all restrictions and discriminations imposed on the Jews without demanding changes in their occupational or education systems. The Jews themselves would take the necessary measures "toward culture" in response to the far-reaching change in the general climate, willingly adopting the values of tolerance in gratitude for the "love" showered upon them. Once the Jews were recognized as desirable members of civil society, no further need would exist to maintain the community's autonomy. A secular judicial system would prevail, for example, and judges—either Jews or Christians, but first and foremost men of conscience—would hear disputes between Jews according to Jewish law as well as civil disputes. To fears that the Jews' commitment to the prophecy of renewed settlement in the Land of Israel precluded them from being completely loyal to the country granting them citizenship, Mendelssohn responded that substantial improvement in living conditions would result in the suppression of messianic expectations. Citizenship and tolerance would encourage the Jews to confine such expectations to the synagogue, making them irrelevant to the Jews' lives in the European context:

> The hoped-for return to Palestine, which troubles Herr Michaelis so much, has no influence on our conduct as citizens. This is confirmed by experience wherever Jews are tolerated. In part, human nature accounts for it—only the enthusiast would not love the soil on which he thrives, and if he holds contradictory religious opinions, he reserves them for church and prayer and does not think more of them.

The fulfillment of Mendelssohn's liberal and pluralistic dream of citizenship also depended on surmounting another grave obstacle—the Jews' devotion to the autonomic organization of their community. Much to Mendelssohn's regret, this system was fully supported in Dohm's plan. Although Dohm demanded a series of far-reaching changes in the Jews' economic, occupational, and educational systems, he left undisturbed the existing state policy granting different groups different rights of organization, legislation, and autonomy. Dohm held that if the state were to gradually grant civil rights to Jews, the current system of autonomy—under which Jewish legal proceedings took place in accordance with Jewish law and the authority of Jewish "ecclesiastical society" included the right of religious excommunication—could continue. Mendelssohn thought this system an insufferable affront to the principles of the Enlightenment, the value of religious tolerance, and the liberty of the Jews in his ideal state: "To introduce church discipline, and yet not impair civil happiness, seems to me a problem, which yet remains for politics to solve." In the Preface he urged the removal of the authority of excommunication from the rabbinical leadership's hands, as one element of his liberal doctrine that would diminish the governing power of any church or clergy.

That the Church could act with impunity "to correct or expel the refractory, and put the stray and deviating again into the right track," Mendelssohn wrote, was unprecedented and unjustifiable. Since his dispute with Lavater more than ten years earlier, Mendelssohn had not permitted himself to give vent to his passion on this issue, or to lose his renowned philosophical patience and composure. Now, though, he was unrestrained:

> I know of no rights over either persons or things, which can possibly have any connection with, or dependence on doctrines. . . . Still less do I know of any right and power over opinions, that are supposed to be conferred by religion. . . . True divine religion arrogates no dominion over thought and

opinion. . . . True divine religion needs neither arms nor fingers for its use; it is all spirit and heart . . . with what conscience can we deny entrance to dissenters, separatists, mis-believers, or sectarians, and deprive them of the benefit of that edification. . . . Doors of the house of rational devotion require neither bars nor bolts. There is nothing locked up within, and, therefore, no occasion to be particular in admitting from without. . . . I shall forbear speaking of the danger there is in entrusting *any one* with the power of excommunicating—with the abuse inseparable from the right of anathema, as indeed with every other form of church discipline, or ecclesiastical power. Alas! It will require ages yet, before the human race shall have recovered from the blows which those monsters inflicted on it. I can imagine no possibility of bridling false religious zeal; as long as it sees that road open before it.

Did Mendelssohn consider himself a dissident who was liable to find himself on trial before the Jewish ecclesiastical authorities—like Baruch Spinoza, say, who had been excommunicated some 130 years earlier in Amsterdam? Did he regard ecclesiastic authority as an opening for the perpetuation of the tyrannical rule of the church in the Age of Enlightenment as well? Did he fear violation of the individual's freedom of thought? Did he fear the dissipation of the dream of the liberal civil state that does not interfere in the beliefs and opinions of its members in any way? It would appear that all these fears helped inspire his uncompromising stand against Dohm's plan in its support for the continued autonomy of the Jewish community, including its elders' right to excommunicate anyone who strayed. Toward the end of the Preface, however, Mendelssohn extended his demand for religious tolerance from the external battleground of the German state to the internal battleground of the rabbis. Grave apprehensions weighed on him in the wake of reports from Prague and Hamburg-Altona that the *Bi'ur* might be banned. Shortly before Mendelssohn wrote the Preface, rumors reached Berlin that Rabbi Raphael Kohen had persecuted a Jew from his community who had defied the community's authority. The German writer and satirist August Cranz, a fervent devotee of the Enlightenment, had written about the affair, to Mendelssohn's embarrassment. While he was struggling to eradicate prejudice and demand religious tolerance of Christians toward Jews, a rabbi was flaunting the religious fanaticism of Jews against Jews. This persecution constituted further proof for Mendelssohn that all forms of ecclesiastical authority were intolerable.

Mendelssohn certainly did not mean for the state authorities to interfere in this affair or to revoke the rabbis' authority by force of law. Such a measure would be contrary to his persistent opposition to the state's interference in the process of citizenship. Rather, his vision—perhaps fairly categorized as wishful thinking—was voluntary relinquishment by ecclesiastic authorities of the right to enforce religious discipline. Mendelssohn concluded the Preface with an emotional call to the rabbis to lead the Jews in adopting the Enlightenment, thus transforming the community into an open organization in which membership was voluntary and coercion obsolete. Mendelssohn called upon the Jewish leadership to relinquish use of the "avenging sword, which madness only thinks it can manage surely." Perhaps, he added, in the past, in the age of religious fanaticism and Jewish persecution at the hands of Christians, Jewish authorities might have found a measure of satisfaction in exploiting their authority to supervise and punish; the unfortunate victim, Mendelssohn acknowledged, at times adopts the methods of his oppressors toward those weaker than himself ("Revenge will be seeking an object; and if it cannot wreak itself on strangers, it even tortures its own flesh and blood"). Perhaps, too, he wrote, those leaders had let themselves be seduced by the prevailing trend in the world and the "error that

religion can be maintained by iron force—doctrines of blessed-
ness inculcated by un-blest persecution." But in the Age of Enlightenment and religious tolerance, there were better examples
to follow. Now, Mendelssohn urged, on the march to liberation
from external slavery, the time had come to forgo internal sub-
jugation:

> The nations are now tolerating and bearing with one an-
> other, while to you also they are showing kindness and for-
> bearance. . . . O, my brethren, follow the example of love, the
> same as you have hitherto followed that of hatred. Imitate
> the virtues of the nations whose vices you hitherto thought
> you must imitate. If you would be protected, tolerated and
> indulged, protect, tolerate, and indulge one another. Love,
> and ye will be beloved.

Would the leaders of the Jewish religion agree to saw off the
branch on which they were sitting and voluntarily relinquish
their status and authority? Would they voluntarily dismantle
the traditional community's mechanisms of supervision and
autonomy? History shows, contrary to Mendelssohn's dream,
that the interference of the modern centralist government was
in fact the main cause of the decline of Jewish autonomy. As
the state, motivated by increased efficiency and reinforced sov-
ereignty, gradually took judicial and tax-collecting authority
out of the hands of the community, the traditional leadership
lost its power. Mendelssohn had read the map correctly and
seen that the Jews were on the road to more modern modes of
existence. He foresaw the collapse of the old community organization model but was unable to persuade leaders to take the
initiative for the inevitable change.

In the years during which enlightened scholars and writers
and senior officials in Germany heatedly debated the "Jewish
question," Mendelssohn remained ever sensitive to fluctuations
in public opinion. The renowned Jewish philosopher, who in-

sisted on characterizing himself as an outside observer, actually played a key role in the public discourse of the 1780s, and he was undoubtedly perceived by many as the spokesman of the Jews. Every word he published was valued by the enlightened intellectual public that followed him, read him, and considered his opinions. Mendelssohn took into account the new and surprising voices that introduced the values of the Enlightenment to the public discourse, demanding that those values inform the status of the Jews in the country, but he also took into consideration the intensity of the burdensome and turbid residues of past suffering—prejudices, anti-Jewish images, suspicions, and Christian religious fanaticism. He called upon his Christian readers to reexamine their collective memory and the deeply ingrained negative stereotypes of the Jew, and to do some serious soul searching. In the Preface, published in 1782, the extent to which this liberal Jewish philosopher from Berlin sought the complete triumph of the Enlightenment is evident, but also evident is the depth of his skepticism concerning this possibility. He was plagued by apprehensions just as optimism was on the rise in the circles of enlightened Christian and Jewish men. His dreams of enlightenment, humanism, tolerance, and brotherly love were repeatedly disrupted by nightmares of religious fanaticism, the iron grip of prejudice, persecution, and ostracism from without and within, and his mood swung from one extreme to the other.

7

---◆·◆·◆---

Jerusalem: *The Road to Civic Happiness*

IN 1782 Mendelssohn's friend Napthtali Herz Wessely published an open letter, *Divrei Shalom ve-Emet* (Words of peace and truth), that caused consternation in the rabbinical elite. Mendelssohn anxiously followed the furor stirring Jewish public opinion in the wake of the Wessely affair, which posed a particularly serious challenge to his belief in religious tolerance. In contrast with Mendelssohn's moderate and reserved response to the Austrian Emperor Josef II's Edict of Tolerance, Wessely enthusiastically welcomed the unprecedented window of opportunity that had been opened to Jews. Renewal of the debate on the question of the Jews, the expansion of Enlightenment in Europe, Dohm's proposals for naturalization of the Jews in their countries, the reforms in Jewish education demanded by Josef II, the internal initiatives manifested in the *Bi'ur* project, and the establishment of the new school in Berlin—all these developments struck Wessely as elements of a single, welcome trend. He thought that a turnabout of historic significance was taking place in relations between Jews and Christians, Jews and the modern state, Jews and the benevolent monarchs. From that moment, Wessely contended, Jews could no longer sit on their hands waiting passively; rather, they must take action. Wessely appealed to the community leaders, rabbis, and all Jews concerned with the fate of their people to support the Austrian emperor's demands, and in particular to establish voluntarily a system of reformed Jewish schools.

In *Divrei Shalom ve-Emet* Wessely set out the ideology of the Jewish Enlightenment for the first time. He outlined detailed plans for the modern Jewish school: a balanced curriculum combining religious study ("the teachings of God," as he put it) and general subjects in the humanities, natural sciences, and foreign languages ("the teaching of man"), with specialized teachers and careful organization of the structures of lessons, classrooms, and textbooks. Moreover, his proposed revolution in the traditional education system of the *heder* and *yeshiva* was just one manifestation of a worldview focused on the Jews' worthy place in society and country, and on the image of the ideal Jew. In Wessely's view, the nascent modern state of affairs in enlightened and tolerant Europe opened new opportunities in the economy, social relations, civil status, and even the Jews' state of mind. From now on Wessely's ideal Jew could and should be not only a believer, loyal to traditions and connected to the community, but also a devoted citizen and happy person capable of enjoying his life. In *Divrei Shalom ve-Emet* he bitterly criticized the flaws in traditional education, including poor teaching standards, and decried the limitations of a world of knowledge restricted to the religious library. He demanded the speedy establishment of new systems representing "the proper order."

Without being fully aware of all the implications of his proposals, Wessely had fomented a stormy cultural-social revolution. In *Divrei Shalom ve-Emet* he announced the opening of the modern era in the history of the Jews, proposed a new ideal of a Jew, whose world and life would be shaped by the unique and the universal alike—a Jew who is both citizen and man—and declared the rabbinical elite unworthy of continuing to dictate life in Jewish society. In this manifesto was born the self-awareness of the modern Jew, conscious of his modernity and determined to effect cultural change. This awareness was to nourish almost every Jewish movement for reform and revolution in the years ahead. Yet no less significant was Wessely's initiative to enlist Jewish public opinion in support of his primary Jewish Enlightenment program. When important rabbis realized that Wessely had circumvented their authority, their reaction was predictable and emphatic. The rabbis, who represented the leadership elite that for generations had maintained sole responsibility for the teaching and guidance of the Jewish population, could not tolerate the appearance of this maskil competitor. Important rabbis like Ezekiel Landau of Prague in Bohemia and David Tevele of Lissa in western Poland delivered acerbic sermons in which they castigated Wessely for his presumption in trying to circumvent them to engage Jewish public opinion, and vilified the insolence of an unordained Jew who proposed alternatives to traditional education that threatened a mortal blow to the value of Torah study. The rabbis sought to exclude Wessely from the community. Wessely defended himself in a series of open letters, attempting to enlist the support of moderate rabbis from the elite. But Rabbi Landau formed a broad front of rabbis who would stand fast against this threat to their position.

Mendelssohn credited Wessely's good intentions and approved of the aims and direction of the reformed Jewish education project proposed in *Divrei Shalom ve-Emet*. But he did not share the revolutionary spirit of the intellectuals and the public outcry—rapidly developing into one of the earliest Jewish

Kulturkampfen—placed him in a quandary. Only a few weeks had elapsed since he had expressed the hope near the end of his Preface to *Vindiciae Judaeorum* that religious tolerance would be a guiding principle under which the Jewish leadership would voluntarily relinquish its authority for punishment. Now Wessely brought a similar proposal to general public opinion. Mendelssohn was troubled by rumors of the burning of copies of *Divrei Shalom ve-Emet*, of threats to its author, and of pressure on Rabbi Zvi Hirsch Levin of Berlin to take punitive measures, even to excommunicate Wessely. Jewish society was facing a public Enlightenment test that was closely monitored by government officials and the press alike, and the persecution of Wessely seemed clear evidence that the leadership had failed that test. In an urgent letter to David Friedländer at the beginning of the affair, Mendelssohn expressed his outrage and anger about this crude demonstration of intolerance by the rabbis. "What will the Christians have to say about this? What will they think when we exert force on this writer and seek to prevent him from expressing his thoughts?" Mendelssohn asked in angry confusion. He had fought to achieve for the Jews fulfillment of the Enlightenment's values of freedom and tolerance, and now Jews were themselves behaving contrary to those values. "Generally," Mendelssohn continued in his letter, "in the land of our most gracious King [Friedrich II] any writer, be he circumcised or uncircumcised, enjoys every possible freedom," and it was inconceivable that Jews themselves would curtail that freedom. Mendelssohn expressed a willingness to meet with Rabbi Levin and attempt to reason with him, but was reluctant to enter into confrontation with him. He wondered whether it might be better if someone else explained to him that in his response to the pressure exerted on him by his fellow rabbis from other communities, he should contend that freedom of the press was a right assured to all in Germany, and that no one should be prevented from expressing his opinion.

Throughout the Wessely affair Mendelssohn worked vigorously behind the scenes in his friend's defense, attempting at the same time to minimize the affair's damage to the image of the Jewish nation as seekers of tolerance. He asked the Jewish community of Trieste, Italy, to help Wessely obtain the support of relatively moderate rabbis interested in the study of general subjects and foreign languages. In several personal letters he assailed the "heartless" individuals who had undertaken a campaign of vengeance against Wessely. "God knows that my heart turned over in my breast," Mendelssohn wrote to Joseph Galico, secretary of the Trieste community and Wessely supporter. He lamented the injustice that had been done and settled scores with the rabbis incapable of admitting their failure in leading the community:

> My close friend Rabbi Herz Wessely, may he enjoy long life, who is known by all who fear God and revere His name for his rare writing and great erudition in Torah and wisdom and fear of God and love of His creatures, and who has always walked the path of righteousness and not strayed to the ways of perversity either in word or deed as all his books will testify, and now in *Divrei Shalom ve-Emet* he has arisen to strengthen weak hands and awaken sleepers from the slumber of the indolent, and he has been assailed by men of hatred who inflict suffering on him and persecute him, as if, Heaven forbid, he has incited all the People of Israel against their heavenly Father. To this pass has come the folly of the heartless who know not left from right, or the malice of those who disagree and seek to flaunt their defects.

It was clear almost from the outset that the focus of the Wessely controversy had shifted from reform of the Jewish education system to the elite maskilims' challenge to the jealously guarded authority of the rabbinical elite. Wessely tried to defend himself along the lines of Mendelssohn's public appeal to the rabbis in the Preface to *Vindiciae Judaeorum*. It seemed, in fact, that Mendelssohn might suffer for his uncompromising stand at Wessely's side. Rabbi Landau wrote to the rabbi of Berlin, Zvi Hirsch Levin, that Mendelssohn's Preface provided indisputable proof of his compromised loyalty to the Jewish religion: "Now I see that every offense we have found him to be guilty of was all true. He has declared of himself that he has no share in the God of Israel not in His Torah, and that every man may do as his heart desires. Moreover, he has printed his words in a foreign tongue, and to the monarchs he has spoken ill of the Sages of Israel." Such bitter criticism seems to have been confined to correspondence between the rabbis; no one dared utter such charges in public. Still, the figure of Mendelssohn as a dangerous heretic, a threat to the rabbis' authority and to the very foundations of the Jewish religion, was preserved in the rabbinical tradition. Mendelssohn, who was aware of what was being said and written, did not flinch from the vicious barbs, some of which were directed at him personally. His anxiety over the affair's implications for the principle of tolerance made him extraordinarily active in resisting the religious fanaticism displayed by the rabbis persecuting Wessely. Together with David Friedländer, Daniel Itzig, and others from the leadership of the Berlin Jewish community, Mendelssohn sent a letter to the communities of Lissa and Posen addressing the threats of excommunication against Wessely. Mendelssohn and his colleagues presented an ultimatum to the leaders of those communities: silence their rabbis and demand a public apology and a retraction of the excommunication threat, or the letter writers would ask the Polish authorities to intervene in the affair. "We shall do everything in our power to save the soul of our friend from his foes," wrote the seven Berliners who signed the letter, adding a vague threat: "and who knows where this matter might end."

This unprecedented mobilization to Wessely's defense of

representatives of the Berlin Jewish community's economic and intellectual elite further underscored the dividing line between the enlightened Jewish camp and the rabbinical elite. As the affair continued to filter into Christian public opinion, and fears grew for Wessely's defenders that it would seriously harm the image of the Jews, Mendelssohn and his allies pressed the threat of legal action against the fanatical rabbis. And indeed, fears of an unhappy outcome were well grounded. Secular critics posed the question: is the rabbis' conduct not incontrovertible proof of the weakness of the Jews' principle of religious tolerance? And does this weakness not indicate a profound contradiction and a fundamental failure of Mendelssohn's beliefs?

The German writer and satirist August Cranz voiced just such concerns in the summer of 1782, when he wrote two articles on the tension among the Jews. In the first he reported on the Wessely affair as an example of religious fanaticism, persecution of an innocent victim, and injustice that contradicted the aims and values of the Enlightenment. In the second, he criticized Mendelssohn's Preface to *Vindiciae Judaeorum*. A year earlier Cranz had upset Mendelssohn by reporting on Rabbi Raphael Kohen's persecution of a nonconforming Jew in Hamburg-Altona. Now Cranz's articles backed Mendelssohn into a corner and presented him, thirteen years after the Lavater affair, with another complex Enlightenment test: how could his contention that Judaism rejects coercion in matters of faith and opinion withstand the rabbis' campaign of religious fanaticism against Wessely?

Particularly grave from Mendelssohn's point of view was a public challenge in a short tract written by Cranz but published anonymously in Berlin in June 1782. *Das Forschen nach Licht und Recht* (The search for light and right) seared Mendelssohn's heart, still scarred from the Lavater affair. Whereas Lavater had exploited something Mendelssohn had said about Jesus in a private conversation, Cranz seized on the Preface to

Vindiciae Judaeorum, weighing Mendelssohn's adherence to the Jewish religion against his declared opposition to religious coercion. Anyone reading the Preface, Cranz wrote sarcastically, might be tempted to wish that Lavater would make another attack on Mendelssohn so as to finally effect the conversion the earlier writer had foreseen, or at least to provoke Mendelssohn to refute a religion that he seemed either unwilling or unable to embrace fully. But unlike Lavater, Cranz did not act out of missionary zeal. A deist himself, Cranz was a bitter critic of religious fanaticism of any kind, an enthusiastic supporter of Jews' rights, an opponent of civil restriction and discrimination against them, and a great admirer of Mendelssohn. After Mendelssohn's death, Cranz wrote of him: "He remained a loyal Jew until his dying day. . . . He was a good and noble man who did not forget the human being in the Jew and the Christian." His wish was that Mendelssohn should stand with him in the struggle of the anticlerical enlightened against superstition, ecclesiastical authority, and religious coercion. To this end Mendelssohn should, in his opinion, express his qualms regarding the fanatical characteristics of the Jewish religion and retract the declarations of his adherence to "the faith of the forefathers." This was an Enlightenment test unlike the one Lavater had engineered. It was not a renewal of the Jewish-Christian controversy in a different guise; this time it was an inclusive test of adapting Judaism to the basic principles of the Enlightenment, on which Cranz and Mendelssohn were in agreement.

But the new attack opened old wounds, and convinced Mendelssohn that the account in public opinion opened by the Lavater affair had not been settled. Again his every word was being scrutinized with the aim of exploiting his weak points, backing him into a corner, and confronting him with a choice between Judaism and the Enlightenment, not to mention between Judaism and Christianity. Mendelssohn—in whose worldview religion was the individual's personal business and a matter of his own conscience, and religion was independent from state or community—was being called upon for a public accounting of his religious identity. Cranz demanded: "The people are justly worthy of you providing them with a reason for the great disparity between you and the faith of your forefathers, or that you announce the cause preventing you from publicly accepting Christianity." Cranz held that the Jewish religion, at least as embodied in rabbinical law, was based upon a system of proscriptions and punishments. Only political circumstances, not principles of faith, prevented Jews of the Diaspora from imposing the heavy penalties of ecclesiastical law upon those deviating from religious orthodoxy. How, then, could Mendelssohn, who denied the authority of such religious punishment, uphold the religion of his forefathers and at the same time disrupt its very fabric? For Cranz, Mendelssohn's denial of the right of excommunication was a de facto disassociation from the faith of his forefathers: "My dear Mr. Mendelssohn, you have, in your remarkable preface, wrenched the cornerstone, by stripping, in dry words, the synagogue of its original power; by denying it the right of expelling from the congregation of the holy, the backslider from the Faith of your Forefathers." It would be better, Cranz went on, if Mendelssohn were to acknowledge that the inferior status of the Jews derived not only from Christian prejudices but also from laws of Judaism—for instance, the Sabbath observance—that perpetuate the Jewish community's isolationism and preclude it from taking an equal part in civic life. From now on, Cranz wrote, Mendelssohn, in order to further the aims of the Enlightenment, to be consistent in his rejection of the clerics' power, and to promote the advancement of the Jews' naturalization, must dare to take the next logical step: "You, good Mr. Mendelssohn, have renounced the religion of your forefathers. One step more, and you will become one of us." Toward the end of his tract Cranz added an extra challenge: that Mendelssohn become his people's great liberator, that he help the Jews cast off the paralyzing shackles of religious law in order to rise anew as free men, to shed the restrictions against uniting with their neighbors and become part of a civic society holding different beliefs. Cranz viewed abrogation of the Jews' religious precepts as a sine qua non for the realization of the Enlightenment's vision of the future, and he called upon Mendelssohn to take a great revolutionary step in leading his people into the Enlightenment project.

But nothing was further from Mendelssohn's mind than responding to this public call and taking the road to Jewish civic happiness recommended by Cranz. By the 1790s, a decade after Mendelssohn's death, radical maskilim and deists like David Friedländer and Lazarus Bendavid came to promote legal emancipation in exchange for abrogation of religious precepts, but for Mendelssohn, observance of the precepts was integral to Judaism. At the end of 1782 he began a written response to Cranz's challenge. In *Jerusalem; Or, On Religious Power and Judaism*, he outlined a totally different path to civic happiness. Only when the idea of religious tolerance became deeply rooted in the hearts of civic leaders and religious leaders could a dignified existence be guaranteed the Jews under the conditions of the "modern situation."

Like his "Letter to Deacon Lavater," *Jerusalem* was written in a tremendous flurry of emotions and with a feeling of affront. Mendelssohn apparently thought "The Search for Light and Right" had been written by the apostate Joseph von Sonnenfels, who occupied a senior post in the Austrian government. Consequently, he thought that the tract represented the position of government and church officials and revealed the hidden intentions behind the emperor's tolerance policy. In any event, his feelings were unmistakable—the claims made against him,

Mendelssohn wrote, had pierced his heart. The notes emanating from *Jerusalem* were notes of despair. The moment was fast approaching, Mendelssohn wrote, when he would have to stop playing by the rules and dismiss altogether the tenuous hopes of naturalization encouraged by Lessing, Dohm, and Joseph II. If the debate on the question of the Jews had reached the point of the disgraceful deal proposed in "The Search for Light and Right"—naturalization of the Jews in exchange for their relinquishing their religious laws—then he, as seemingly the sole spokesman for the Jews in that public discourse, wished to announce that the Jews had no choice but to waive naturalization. Tolerance and the principles of the Enlightenment dictated that the Jews' emancipation from civic oppression was a right, not a transaction for which payment could be collected.

Jerusalem was another of Mendelssohn's works that he wrote not as an independent, intentional enterprise but out of a feeling of necessity. He continued to proclaim that he much preferred to discuss the issue with scholars and philosophers, not amid the judgment, suspicion, and expectations native to the public context. Still, confronted by those who would undermine the foundations of his beliefs, he tried to prove the justness of his cause: to show that Judaism possesses the potential of enlightenment, and thus that his dual commitment to Judaism and to liberal, tolerant, and rational thinking was not a contradiction. Nor was Cranz alone in demanding of him an ordered response on the question of the Jews and religious tolerance; even such a good friend as Hennings had written him in disappointment after the Wessely affair: "The Bible is replete with proof of how intolerant the Jews were." Hennings even made a proposal that was not far from that of Cranz:

> Why do we even need Judaism or Christianity? We possess doctrines common to all the faiths and commonsense mandates their acceptance. Should we disseminate their

knowledge then we are strengthening the spirit of tolerance. Without general enlightenment there is a constant risk that tolerance will suffer from the poison of factionalism. . . . Let us hope that as one we shall worship the one and only God.

An adversary of a different stripe was the military chaplain Daniel Ernst Mörschel of Berlin, who added a short epilogue to Cranz's tract. Mörschel claimed that the resolute campaign conducted by Mendelssohn against religious coercion proved that he was nothing but a deist, and thus an enemy of the revealed religions. He chided Mendelssohn once and for all to tell the world candidly: was he a Jew or a Christian, or perhaps neither? Mendelssohn found himself assailed on all sides— Lavater had left hanging the wish of the Christian faithful that Mendelssohn would in the end see the light and convert; Rabbi Jacob Emden had told him privately that many doubted his faith in Judaism; Rabbi Ezekiel Landau suspected him of being an Epicurean; and now Mörschel branded him a deist. As the doubts about the degree of his commitment to traditional Judaism mounted, enlightened public opinion was full of demands that he define his identity. As the historian Michael Meyer wrote: "*Jerusalem* was above all a personal defense of Mendelssohn's own existence and the goals of his life."

Jerusalem was Mendelssohn's most important, influential, and enduring work. It was written only some three years before his death; in the words of his biographer Alexander Altmann, "It was the final hour before the gate of his life was locked, in which he wrote a book expressing his personality in all its force." It was also the only book for which Mendelssohn received a fee. His son Joseph wrote:

> I heard from my late father that until 1783 he never received a fee for his writing, only presents of good books that were occasionally given to him by the publisher gentlemen. *Jerusalem* was published by a young publisher called [Friedrich]

Maurer ... who surprised him with a fee of 100 Louis d'or. This sum of money was the only golden fruit he harvested from his literary work all his life.

He wrote the book over a period of eight months, from the end of the summer of 1782 to the early spring of 1783. Cranz's harsh and incisive words—"You, good Mr. Mendelssohn, have renounced the religion of your forefathers"—reverberated in his mind, strengthening his resolve to explain his adherence to the Jewish religion, and at the same time the echoes of the Wessely affair underscored the dangers of homegrown religious fanaticism. As Mendelssohn began writing *Jerusalem*, the Berlin Jewish community was in turmoil after its rabbi, Zvi Hirsch Levin, driven by the pressures of the Wessely affair, had resigned and fled the city in secret. In his letter of resignation Rabbi Levin complained that Cranz, abetted by members of the Berlin Jewish community, had brought down shame upon the Jews by publicizing the affair.

Just as the English philosopher John Locke's *A Letter Concerning Toleration*, published in 1689, had become the basic treatise in European discourse on religious tolerance, *Jerusalem*, which Mendelssohn published some one hundred years later, became the most important treatise of the Jewish Enlightenment on this issue. It was the point of departure for the Jewish discourse, which thereafter had to confront the question of how Jewish identity could be reconciled with the Modern Era—how, in short, the Jewish collective could continue to exist. The work had two objectives: to reiterate that the ecclesiastical establishments must surrender their authority to impose coercive discipline on the faithful, and to prove that loyalty to Jewish religious precepts continued to bind all Jews, and was compatible with loyalty to the principle of religious tolerance.

Regarding the central question of relations between church and state, Mendelssohn adopted Locke's definitions but stopped short of his radical solution. Both men distinguished between the various spheres of responsibility of these two institutions, but Locke contended that freedom of conscience could be ensured only by a separation of church and state. Far more than Locke, Mendelssohn was assailed by demons that threatened the possibility of achieving the "felicity of social life." His liberal solution was designed to ensure not only individual liberty but also the stability and morality of society. Mendelssohn identified four banes to the well-being of human society: a tyrannical regime that rode roughshod over man's natural rights and suffocated liberty; civic anarchy in a torn society in which liberty is unrestricted; religious fanaticism nourished by prejudice, hypocrisy, delusion, superstition, and the cunning of priests; and denial of the existence of God, which leads to the collapse of morality. Because religious impulses help to shape public order, Mendelssohn held, the state cannot remain totally indifferent to its citizens' participation at least in the essence of natural religion. "Hence, every civil society," he contended, "would do well to let neither of them, neither fanaticism nor atheism, take root and spread." In the philosophical debate on whether an apostate can be a moral person, Mendelssohn's position was unequivocal: without belief in God, divine providence, and reward and punishment in the next world, a civic society based on justice, loyalty, and morality cannot exist. The state is therefore obliged to a certain minimal degree of involvement in the sphere of the church. Absolute separation between the transitory interests of human beings and their eternal interests is not, in his view, correct; in the end the obligation of ensuring man's happiness is imposed upon the state: "The state, to be sure, is to see it from afar that no doctrines are propagated which are inconsistent with the public welfare; doctrines which, like Epicureanism, undermine the foundations on which the felicity of social life is based."

By contrast, on the issue of the use of coercion by the

ecclesiastical establishment, Mendelssohn presented a radical and uncompromising position in *Jerusalem*. He was, in fact, fighting for separation of church and state—for annulment of the criterion of religious affiliation in all matters pertaining to citizens' rights in the state—and for weakening ecclesiastical power. In his opinion, there is an essential difference between church and state: "The state gives orders and coerces, religion teaches and persuades. The state prescribes laws, religion commandments. The state has physical power and uses it when necessary; the power of religion is love and beneficence." Religion and the right of compulsion are contradictory, and the real battle for the principle of religious tolerance must be prosecuted with all vigor and resolve against the claim of the clerics to use the right of coercion against members of the church. Here, again, Mendelssohn the liberal rages against any attempt to force opinions and religious beliefs, or to ostracize those who deviate from orthodoxy:

> [Religion] does not prod men with an iron rod; it guides them with bonds of love. It draws no avenging sword, dispenses no temporal goods, assumes no right to any earthly possessions, and claims no external power over the mind. Its weapons are reason and persuasion; its strength is the divine power of truth. . . . Excommunication and right to banish, which the state may occasionally permit itself to exercise, are diametrically opposed to the spirit of religion.

Mendelssohn made an emotional plea to his readers, in a universal spirit: "Reader! To whatever visible church, synagogue or mosque you may belong! See if you do not find more true religion among the host of excommunicated than among the far greater host of those who excommunicated them. . . . To expel a dissident from the church is like forbidding a sick person to enter a pharmacy." The question arises: are not these unwavering opinions of Mendelssohn's, the lover of liberty and tolerance, clear evidence of the justness of Cranz's contention? Is not this manner of presenting religion consistent with Cranz's barbed challenge to Mendelssohn: "How can you . . . profess attachment to the religion of your forefathers, while you are shaking its fabric, by impugning the ecclesiastical code established by Moses in consequence of divine revelation?" Mendelssohn rejected any such implication. The claim that he sought to destroy his religion, he wrote, was disgraceful and personally hurtful; it had no place in the polite discourse of scholars. He acknowledged that many Jews perceive Judaism as a religion based upon coercion, punishment, and grave "ecclesiastical justice" but denied that true Judaism conforms to those criteria. If indeed he credited that perception, Mendelssohn continued, then the conflict between it and his own reasoning would make him a skeptic and thus impose silence upon him. Mendelssohn thus washed his hands of the conduct of rabbis such as David Tevele of Lissa and Raphael Kohen of Hamburg-Altona in the Wessely affair. Their religious fanaticism was not "true Judaism," which is essentially tolerant. In conversations with guests in his salon, Mendelssohn was often blunter in his criticism of the state of Judaism. One admirer, Sophie Becker from Courland, recorded Mendelssohn's words in her journal: "True Judaism is not to be found anywhere. Fanaticism and superstition are with us to a most abhorrent degree."

As to the option of conversion to Christianity, Mendelssohn replied sarcastically to Cranz that the notion of fleeing from his collapsing religion to Christianity was implausible: "If it be true that the cornerstones of my house are dislodged, and the structure threatens to collapse, do I act wisely if I remove my belongings from the lower to the upper floor for safety? Am I more secure there? Now Christianity, as you know, is built upon Judaism, and if the latter falls, it must necessarily collapse with it into one heap of ruins." Here Mendelssohn reached the core of *Jerusalem* and clearly defined the unique-

ness of Judaism and the borders separating it from Christianity:
"I believe that Judaism knows of no revealed religion in the
sense in which Christians understand this term." Christianity,
he wrote, is based on divine revelation of the principles of faith,
while Judaism, in contrast, is based on the revelation of law.
Mosaic Law incorporates neither coercion regarding faith nor
threats of punishment to ensure belief in dogma. It therefore
falls into line with the liberal idea of man's liberty. Reiterating
the belief he had expressed in his debate with Lavater, Mendelssohn asserted that the doctrines of natural religion ("eternal truths")—the existence of God, divine providence, and
the immortality of the soul—is universal and rational. In other
words, any man can acknowledge these doctrines by means of
the tools given to him by God: rational thinking and observation of nature without the mediation of divine revelation and
without the guidance of religious teachers. In contrast with the
claims voiced for generations in the Christian-Jewish polemic,
Mendelssohn proposed that it is Christianity that is extremely
limited, because it preaches a dogma opposing reason, and because it claims to provide its believers with exclusive access to
salvation. Judaism, on the other hand, does not demand belief
in something that is senseless and manifests tolerance in ac-
knowledging the possibility of salvation and happiness for all
human society.

In *Jerusalem* Mendelssohn developed this basic idea in
clear and incisive words: "All these excellent propositions are
presented to the understanding, submitted to us for consideration, without being forced upon our belief. . . . Faith is not
commanded, for it accepts no other commands than those that
come to it by way of conviction." In Judaism, Mendelssohn
contended, there is no agreement on the principles of faith and
no one is sworn to belief in dogma. In the Middle Ages various
philosophers—Maimonides, for example—proposed different
principles of faith, but their suggestions never became binding.

Therefore the uniqueness of the Jewish religion is in divine law, the practical commandments. In the historical context in which Mendelssohn wrote *Jerusalem* this was not only a theological notion but part of a polemical, challenging worldview. It was with good reason that Mendelssohn chose the symbolic title *Jerusalem*. His attackers, Cranz and Mörschel, thought that his criticism of religious coercion freed him from the commitment to the laws and ceremonies of practical Judaism, and that he was moving closer to the Christians who "no longer pinned true worship of God either in Samaria or Jerusalem" but rooted it in spirit and belief. But Mendelssohn declared, in candid opposition, his adherence to the ritual, the ceremonies, and the practical commandments that are symbolized by Jerusalem as the setting of the ancient ritual of the Jewish people. *Jerusalem* was the code word for Mendelssohn's rejection of any notion of conversion and his declaration of loyalty to the Jewish religion and its commandments.

Baruch Spinoza, too, the ostracized seventeenth-century Jewish philosopher with whose "Theological-Political Treatise" Mendelssohn had conducted a covert dialogue, had viewed the Mosaic Laws of the ancient state of the Hebrews as the essence of the uniqueness of Judaism. Yet a deeper reading of *Jerusalem* reveals that for Mendelssohn the significance of the laws was far broader than the political role assigned to them by Spinoza. Even if the Torah, "the divine book that we received through Moses," is supposed to be a code of law whose rules must be observed in temporal life, it also includes "ordinances, rules of life, and prescriptions, it also includes, as is well known, an inexhaustible treasure of rational truths and religious doctrines which are so intimately connected with the laws that they form but one entity." The distinction between religious principles and religious laws is not clear-cut and perhaps does not even exist. The connection between the commandments and the truths of reason is, in fact, one of the reasons of the commandments: "All laws refer to, or are based upon, eternal truths of reason, or remind us of them, and rouse us to ponder them." The practical commandments preserve the abstract concepts of religion through tangible, everyday deeds. Furthermore, the Torah and its commandments shape the Jewish nation. Contrary to later criticism that Mendelssohn, by positioning Judaism on the commandments, denied the Jews any claim to a coherent set of national characteristics, he here associated observance of the commandments with a way of life that embraced a specific national meaning, if not precisely in its modern political sense. The entire Torah is the nation's most precious asset, Mendelssohn declared: the historical stories of the beginnings of the nation are "the foundation of the national union," and observance of the commandments brings "national felicity" to all and personal happiness to each member of the nation. And if that were not enough, Mendelssohn also ascribed a key role to the commandments in the Jewish mission in history as the people chosen to serve as a shining example to all the nations of the world, the bearer of the ideas of pure religious belief.

In this debate on the significance of the practical commandments, the uniqueness of the Jewish religion, and its superiority over Christianity, was not Mendelssohn evading the knottiest question, that of religious coercion? How else can we explain what is obvious to all readers of Mosaic Law—that a heavy punishment awaits every sinner against God? Toward the end of *Jerusalem* Mendelssohn attempted to deal with this apparent contradiction, which seemed to undercut his claim that Judaism incorporates a doctrine of religious tolerance. This time he found support in Spinoza's idea: in the ancient Hebrew state there was no separation of state and religion because God was the nation's king, the leader of a de facto theocracy—a government of God and the priests. While Mendelssohn had some reservations about this pigeonholing—Spinoza's definition was too rigid, Mendelssohn thought, for the unique phenomenon that was ancient Judaism—he did acknowledge the early Hebrew state as a theocratic regime. In this primal situation, he contended, "every sacrilege against the authority of God, as the lawgiver of the nation, was a crime against the Majesty." Unlike the ecclesiastical authorities, the state authorities are entitled to use force to enforce civil order and state laws. He who reviled God or wickedly broke the Sabbath abrogated a fundamental law of civil society, undermined the state itself, and was therefore worthy of punishment. In the ancient Jewish state coercion was not religious but civil, since punishment was imposed not for an erroneous opinion or lack of belief but for a crime against the state, and even this justified punishment was uncommon. The conditions necessary for a guilty verdict were so circumscribed that in only a few cases was the death sentence passed. In summing up his response to Cranz, Mendelssohn wrote:

> This clearly shows how little one must be acquainted with the Mosaic law and the constitution of Judaism to believe that according to them ecclesiastical right and ecclesiastical power are authorized, or that temporal punishments are to be inflicted for unbelief or erring belief. *The Searcher after Light and Right* [Cranz], as well as Mr. Mörschel, are therefore far removed from the truth when they believe I have abolished Judaism by my rational arguments against ecclesiastical right and ecclesiastical power.

Arrayed against this ideal description of the ancient Jewish state and its theocratic regime stood the reality of Jewish existence in exile over many years. After the destruction of the Temple, a regime based on Mosaic Law had ceased to exist. In Spinoza's opinion, the disappearance of the Kingdom of the Hebrews also freed the Jews of their obligation to obey the commandments, and collective Jewish existence faced dissolution. The continued survival of the Jews was, in his view, pathetic; its existence depended solely on the unifying adhesive of pietи...l superstitions and the mutual hatred of Jews and Gentiles. In contrast, Mendelssohn felt that this historical breaking point actually effected a qualitative quantum leap in the Jewish religion. From this point onward, religious offences could no longer be considered crimes against the state. Religion had extricated itself from an overlap with civil law, and thereafter observance of religious precepts depended on a person's wishes, not any system of threats, coercion, or punishment. From this stage onward Judaism represented the best of Enlightenment values.

In diametrical contrast to Spinoza, Mendelssohn not only denied that severance from state and territory freed one from the obligation of observance of the commandments but insisted that such a condition in fact reinforced the duty to obey the law. Although numerous commandments were irrelevant to Jewish communities in the Diaspora because they involved worship in the Temple and the Land of Israel, it was inconceivable that the rest were obsolete in the absence of a new revelation from the Divine Lawgiver. "In fact, I cannot see how those born into the House of Jacob can in any conscientious manner disencumber themselves of the law," Mendelssohn wrote in one of the book's most salient sentences, "as long as we can point to no such authentic exemption from the law, no sophistry of ours can free us from the strict obedience we owe to the law; and reverence for God draws a line between speculation and practice which no conscientious man may cross." This uncompromising commitment to the commandments, which shut the door not only on religious permissiveness but also on any manner of religious reform, was Mendelssohn's incisive response to all who wondered why he continued to adhere to the commandments.

While this declaration made sense of the way Mendelssohn conducted his life, it did engender questions in later generations from those who sought contradiction, two-facedness, between Moses of Dessau, with his fundamentalist approach to observance of the commandments, and Moses Mendelssohn, the liberal philosopher. Could Mendelssohn have concealed true religious leanings that in fact were closer to those of the deists, the devotees of natural religion, than to those who believed in revealed religion? Could his robust declaration of fidelity have been for public consumption, calculated to deflect suspicion and maintain his status among his Jewish brethren? The consistent position maintained by Mendelssohn on this subject whenever confronted provides no grounds for such speculation. Mendelssohn was clearly unhappy with the way the Jewish religion was perceived by his generation, and as we have seen he invariably criticized religious fanaticism, superstition, and the shift away from "true Judaism." But his belief in tradition and in the duty of devotion to the divine law revealed to the Jews at Mount Sinai, and his defense of the Pentateuch against the criticism of the Christian scholars, cannot be doubted. In *Jerusalem* he further reinforced his embrace of this worldview. Not only did he extend the philosophical debate on the meaning of the commandments—as a sort of hieroglyphics, cryptically guiding the intelligence toward recognition of the divine truths—but he also sought, at the cost of great personal suffering, to reinforce Judaism's defenses against the attacks of the enlightened philosophers.

Jerusalem was written in a deeply pessimistic mood. The confrontations with Lavater, Cranz, and Mörschel had so heightened Mendelssohn's fears of increased missionary activity among theologians and the enlightened alike that he saw a need to state unequivocally that the Jews did not intend to renounce their way of life, including the walls separating them from non-Jews—the dietary laws that restricted social contact and the marriage laws that prevented assimilation. In his defense of devotion to the commandments he therefore placed less emphasis on personal religious experience than on the importance of preserving the "national union" and ensuring "national felicity" in other words, the nation's continued collective existence. In a personal letter in early autumn 1783 to his children's former tutor Herz Homberg, he sought to explain his resolve on the necessity of observing the practical precepts: "The angels of destruction" of reason, he wrote, are still active and are employing against us, the Jews, "a Jesuit stratagem" to make us convert. Against this plot we have no choice but to enlist "all our stiff-neckedness." On the face of it, Mendelssohn declared, the Christians were magnanimously offering the Jews union, but in fact it was deceit:

> They only seek to lure us to cross to that side. They approach us with false steps, they raise their foot and do not move from where they stand. This is the method of unity of wolves who seek so dearly to unite with sheep until they desire to turn the flesh of sheep and lambs into the flesh of wolves. . . . If we listen carefully to these temptations (Heaven help us!) then in fifty years' time all will revert to barbarism.

In the face of these concerns and frustrations, Mendelssohn employed a well-known New Testament verse in proposing to his Jewish audience of *Jerusalem* a pragmatic, cautious, and very pessimistic solution for the tension between the demands of the civil state and those of Jewish religious law: "Render unto Caesar the things which be Caesar's, and unto God the things which be God's." According to him there was no choice but to continue bearing, despite the suffering it involved, the two heavy burdens—the laws of the land and the commandments of religion. This involved a heavy toll, especially when the Jews had not yet attained civil liberty, but it was, in his opinion, the only route to continued existence:

> It is true that, on the one hand, the burden of civil life is made heavier for you on account of the religion to which

you remain faithful, and, on the other hand, the climate and times make the observance of your religious laws in some respects more irksome than they are. Preserve; remain unflinchingly at the post which Providence has assigned to you, and endure everything that happens to you as your lawgiver foretold long ago.

This was also a direct rebuff to Cranz's hope that Mendelssohn would fill the role he had assigned him, that of the leader who would free the Jews from the bonds of religious law.

The final pages of *Jerusalem* evince Mendelssohn's bleak mood; once more he was experiencing nightmares of the return of "barbarism," the code word he employed extensively for all violations, no matter their new and sophisticated guise, of the values of the Enlightenment. In his opinion, for relatively easy conditions to prevail under which the Jews might bear their double burden required religious tolerance and state recognition of the right of the Jewish minority to observe its unique way of life. In the wake of public debate of Dohm's program, Mendelssohn hoped that the universal principles of the Enlightenment might lead to Jewish naturalization without the costs of assimilation that Dohm prescribed. A similarly attractive goal wrapped in threatening means agitated Mendelssohn: a proposal to establish a standard religious faith for all citizens that would bring about an enlightened universal fraternity and abolish once and for all fanaticism and interdenominational hatred. Ever a liberal supporter of pluralism and a defender of freedom of opinion, Mendelssohn positioned himself as a critic from within the Enlightenment itself, sounding a warning prophetic of postmodernist criticism of tyranny in the name of reason.

"Many, indeed, . . . speak of the union of faiths as a very desirable state of affairs," Mendelssohn wrote, "and sadly pity the human race because this pinnacle of felicity cannot be reached by human powers." But this utopian messianic impulse, he added, flouted reason, liberty, and true tolerance. From the desire to root out religious fanaticism sprouted an idea whose implementation depends upon suppression of free will and would simply replace one form of repression with another. In Mendelssohn's view this was a masquerade of hypocrites pretending to tolerance while plotting to hurl human reason "back into the cesspool of barbarism." The moment the principles of this universal union of religions were determined, modern fanaticism would flourish. Whoever dared to challenge these articles of faith and sought to introduce even one small change would be burned at the stake. Therefore, Mendelssohn cautioned his Enlightenment colleagues, "Beware, friends of men, of listening to such sentiments without the most careful scrutiny. They could be snares which fanaticism grown important wants to put in the way of liberty of conscience." Divine providence created a pluralistic world in which thrive different opinions among individual human beings, Mendelssohn reminded his reader. The imposition of a union of religions would be tantamount to tyranny that utterly contradicts the will of God for true tolerance, manifested in a variegated and multicultural humankind.

From Mendelssohn's point of view this was not a theoretical debate on some Enlightenment utopia. The notion of a union of religions threatened his hope that the modern state, guided by the noble desire to naturalize the Jews, might annul the existing correlation of a citizen's rights with his religious affiliation. In the face of the intensifying prospect that retreat from commitment to religious law and abandonment of their separate way of life might be presented as a condition for the Jews' naturalization, Mendelssohn declared in despair: "If civil union cannot be obtained under any other condition than our departing from the laws which we still consider binding on us, then we are sincerely sorry to find it necessary to declare that we must rather do without civil union." This was an extremely pessimistic declaration in the historical context of the prevailing Enlightenment dialogue in German-speaking Europe about the state's attitude towards the Jews. It was for Mendelssohn a rare expression of profound doubt that the Enlightenment could bring about any real relief of the Jews' civic oppression. At the very least, said Mendelssohn almost pleadingly, "Make our burdens as bearable as you can. Regard us, if not as brothers and fellow citizens, at least as fellow men and fellow inhabitants of the land."

The optimism expressed in his 1782 preface to *Vindiciae Judaeorum* that he might live to see "that happy time when attention will be given to human rights in all their proper compass" was replaced by skepticism in *Jerusalem* in 1783. Even in America, one of whose foundation cornerstones was the principle of separation of religion and state, Mendelssohn noted with concern in a footnote, an ominous effort was afoot to establish a state religion. In the shadow of his nightmares about the return of "barbarism" he concluded his book with repeated pleas to the rulers of countries not to interfere in matters of religion, belief, opinion, thought, or expression. A religious opinion is not a matter for the state, he wrote, and civil happiness is not conditional upon it; this is but one of the prejudices of which the state must rid itself. The next generation might possibly attain "that universal tolerance of man for which reason still sighs in vain!" In the meantime, Mendelssohn called upon rulers to "let no one in your states be a searcher of hearts and a judge of thoughts." He presented the minimal conditions required for the Jews' existence in a civil state, even under existing conditions, in Prussia, for instance, under the rule of Friedrich II: "Let everyone be permitted to speak as he thinks, to invoke God after his own manner or that of his fathers, and to seek eternal salvation where he thinks he may find it, as long as he does not disturb public felicity and acts honestly toward the civil laws, toward you and his fellow citizens." Only in the future, after centuries of civilization, would the full vision of tolerance be realized and civil happiness attained, when human beings finally realize that civil discrimination based on religious affiliation must be eliminated.

Mendelssohn's ideological positions on relations between religion and state, his sharp criticism of the various forms of oppression and prejudice, barbarism, superstition, and cruelty, and his unequivocal stand on the values of religious tolerance, humanism, and freedom of thought and expression all made *Jerusalem*, beyond its significance as a statement of defense of the Jewish religion, a masterwork of European Enlightenment culture. Intellectuals' attitudes toward the Jews, in fact, provided an incisive measure of the degree of consistency in Enlightenment practice, and of the goodwill of efforts to employ Enlightenment values practically. At the same time, *Jerusalem* was a Jewish Enlightenment treatise containing ideas through which Mendelssohn sought to position the Jews to encounter the modern world. His criticism of the prejudiced religious fanatics who tarnished pure Judaism, along with his portrayal of "true Judaism"—whose adherents chose it freely, whose principles fell into line with reason and freedom of conscience, whose rabbinical leadership readily surrendered the authority to punish for religious offenses—should have put Mendelssohn on a collision course with the rabbinical elite. This, at least, is what he expected, according to Sophie Becker's quotation in her journal: "If the members of my nation were not such fools they would have stoned me because of my 'Jerusalem,' but people do not understand me."

Although no reader of *Jerusalem* could mistake Mendelssohn's recommendation to his people to continue uncompromisingly observing the practical precepts, he expected an angry reaction from the rabbinical establishment, and he appears to have been somewhat disappointed when it did not materialize. In contrast with his image as a moderate, compromise-seeking man, Mendelssohn possessed considerable fighting spirit when it came to such critical issues as the tension between religious fanaticism and the ideal of religious tolerance. Yet it seems that on this occasion he was immune to censure. His fame, the honor he brought to his coreligionists, and his potential value as a lobbyist conferred special status on him; then too, because *Jerusalem* was published in German and scarcely penetrated Jewish discourse, the rabbinical elite may not have perceived it as a threat to the stability of religious culture.

Still, the rabbis remained extremely sensitive to the manifestations of a new, competing cultural elite. Even while Mendelssohn was writing *Jerusalem*, their attention was still focused on the Wessely affair. While Mendelssohn faced theological and philosophical challenges from European Enlightenment public opinion, Wessely's intention in *Words of Peace and Truth* was to build a foundation in Jewish public opinion for the Haskalah modernization enterprise that would transform education.

Nor was the publication of *Jerusalem* the only event of 1783 to propel the Jewish Enlightenment. At exactly the same time that Mendelssohn was gathering all his intellectual powers to convince people of the need for a liberal, tolerant, and pluralistic society in which the Jews would be entitled to adhere to both their precepts of religious practice and Enlightenment values, an event of revolutionary significance was taking place elsewhere in the Prussian kingdom. In the Königsberg Jewish community Isaac Euchel (1756–1804) founded the Society of Friends of Hebrew Literature. Euchel, a native of Copenhagen who had grown up in Berlin, was a private tutor in the home of the wealthy Friedländer family in Königsberg and a student at the local university who viewed Immanuel Kant as his guide and mentor. At the age of twenty-seven he founded the Jewish Enlightenment's first organization. It was the Haskalah movement's first core association: a group of young Jewish men who were not affiliated with the rabbinical elite but who studied the Pentateuch and its commentators, the Hebrew language, philosophy, history, and science, and who held far-reaching aspirations of rejuvenating Jewish culture. A few months after its establishment the Society first challenged the religious elite's control of the public arena, the Jewish library, and public opinion. Late in 1783 the first editions of *Hame'asef* were published. This monthly Haskalah journal served as a literary and ideological platform and constituted an organizational focal point around which the Haskalah movement took shape.

In 1784 the Freischule printing house in Berlin was established under management of the maskilim, enabling them to disseminate their ideas and compete with the religious library. The cultural agenda, which was essentially literary, restricted the capacity of early maskilic circles to rouse the masses, but the circulation gradually grew. The readers of *Hame'asef*, its distribution agents and contributing writers were dispersed throughout numerous communities from Amsterdam in the west to Vilna in the east, with the majority in communities in central Europe. The *Hame'asef* editorial board moved to Berlin, where a new and broader organizational body was established for the young movement, the Society for the Promotion of Goodness and Justice, whose goal was the foundation of an international Jewish movement with advanced organizational capability that would provide a home for all who identified with the maskilic worldview.

Numerous maskilim, among them Euchel, Joel Brill, Aaron Wolffsohn, and Saul Levin, were involved in collective cultural activities devoted to the modernization of the Jews. While Mendelssohn was presenting his philosophical-political path to "civil happiness," Wessely and Euchel were similarly occupied with the Haskalah enterprise. Mendelssohn posited the transformation of the state as the first and vital step in ensuring the continued existence of the Jews under conditions of the "modern situation," but Wessely, Euchel, and the other maskilim placed the cultural transformation of the Jews at the top of their agenda. Modern education would put an end to the restrictive exclusivity of religious knowledge and values; rationalization of the education system would produce youth trained for life in the civil state while cultivating the Hebrew language, encouraging a new Hebrew literature, and saving and restoring the library of Jewish texts on philosophy, language, and science that had lain neglected since the Middle Ages and the Renaissance. The maskilim perceived this revolution in Jewish education as a contribution to a historical process that would culminate in a dignified, happy life in the Modern Era.

Mendelssohn harbored grave reservations regarding Dohm's program of state intervention to regenerate education among the Jews, but the young maskilim, following Wessely, embraced the main points of Dohm's plan. Euchel, for instance, deplored Jewish ignorance and proposed his own program for fighting all the ills of Jewish society, although in contrast to Dohm he demanded that the rehabilitation and reform of the Jews be in the hands of the Jewish intellectuals and leaders. The young maskilim were united in challenging traditional patterns of Jewish society, especially the monolithic control of the rabbinical elite. Self-aware and armed with a plan for action, the modern intellectuals were poised to engineer a revolution in education.

Mendelssohn played but a marginal role in this cultural project of modernization of the Jews. He was not a partner, either ideologically or practically, in the establishment of the Haskalah movement's institutions, the organization and dissemination of its ideas, the Society of Friends of the Hebrew Language, or the journal *Hame'asef*. As the Haskalah leadership strove to deepen the maskilic influence in Jewish society, Mendelssohn took an interest in the general German journal of his Enlightenment colleagues, the *Berlinische Monatschrift*, and joined the prestigious company of Berlin's leading intellectuals of the 1780s—the secret, elitist Wednesday Society. Although the salon at his Berlin home was also a focal point of pilgrimage for young maskilim from numerous communities inside and outside Germany (especially Poland and Lithuania), who sought his advice and guidance, and although he supported the efforts of the maskilim to develop culture and education, his role in the Haskalah movement was largely passive. When the first editors of *Hame'asef* were looking for a personage of stature in the Jewish community of scholars as a public face of the journal and the movement, they quite naturally approached Wessely, who, like them, was a fervent devotee of the notion of promoting and rejuvenating the Hebrew language and its literature.

Mendelssohn therefore was neither the movement's founder nor the "Father of the Haskalah," neither laying its ideological foundations nor guiding its agenda. Nonetheless, Euchel, who in the 1780s initiated the building of a Jewish Enlightenment movement that would burst into Jewish society as an alternative to the rabbinical elite, was one of Mendelssohn's greatest admirers. More than any other member of that generation, Euchel systematically and studiously shaped the figure of Mendelssohn as a titanic historical personality. Euchel wrote the first Hebrew biography of Mendelssohn, and it appeared first in installments in *Hame'asef*, and later in a special edition. This biography, which included an abridged translation of *Jerusalem*, introduced a Hebrew readership to Mendelssohn's principal ideas, and to a great degree shaped the Mendelssohn myth for generations. Euchel, who first talked with Mendelssohn during his visit to Berlin in 1784, was deeply impressed by his personality and identified with his Enlightenment values. Surprisingly, however, this great admirer did not view Mendelssohn as one of the outstanding maskilim or as an ideological partner. He perceived him only as "a theoretical writer" whose life circumstances and moderate character had kept him away from controversy and made him decline the vital project of the maskilim—rehabilitation of the Jews—that Euchel defined as the role of "the moral physician."

From the failed attempt to publish a Hebrew-language weekly (*Kohelet Musar*), through the *Logical Terms* and the *Bi'ur* enterprise, Mendelssohn had demonstrated his aspiration to contribute to the renewal, the rationalization of Jewish culture, to help cleanse it of superstition and infuse it with enlightened values. His dreams of a tolerant and "true Judaism," his criticism of the rabbis' religious fanaticism and their weapon of excommunication, his support of the persecuted Wessely, and his aspiration to pave "the way toward culture" all attest to Mendelssohn's active support of the thought and values of the Jewish Enlightenment. Founding a movement, though, formulating an ideology—even just establishing a journal and disseminating ideas, to say nothing of a frontal confrontation with the rabbinical elite—was a distant objective. Euchel, who was the most active of all in organizing the Haskalah movement, crowned Mendelssohn head of the movement. In his biography of Mendelssohn he portrayed the model of teacher and students, which for many years afterward was accepted by the Berlin maskilim and historians alike. Yet there were no teacher-student relations between Mendelssohn and the maskilim, and the term *Mendelssohn's disciples* reflects not historical reality but rather the desire of Euchel and other maskilim to adopt their generation's most admired and famed Jew as their spiritual father. Mendelssohn conversed with many people, entertained Jews and Christians in the salon of his home, corresponded with the intensity characteristic of eighteenth-century intellectual life, exchanged ideas, and gave advice, but he was not a teacher, he did not conceive the establishment of the Haskalah movement, and he did not found a school of thought, a system of ideas around which devotees might organize themselves, or that they might seek to develop further.

Nonetheless, Euchel and others—including Friedländer, who after Mendelssohn's death claimed to have been his devoted student—helped to shape Mendelssohn's image. His fervent admirers reinforced his status as an icon, a cultural hero, the revered symbol of the Jewish Enlightenment and of Jewish modernization, even giving Mendelssohn credit for some developments he had never dreamed of. Euchel, in his preface to the abridged translation of *Jerusalem* that he included in his biography of Mendelssohn, called it the author's most magnificent book: "Jerusalem is built as a city in which the Torah, wisdom, judgment and justice are brought together, and who can glorify the magnitude of the virtues of this book, on whose foundations it is worthy and proper that all the learning of righteousness and justice should be built, and from its source will come all the aspects of faith and knowledge." This exceptional book, whose basic philosophical ideas are rooted in the specific historical contexts and tempestuous state of mind that inspired Mendelssohn to write it, indeed provided valuable tools for dealing profoundly with the modern Jewish situation. Yet its influence on the Jewish milieu was not great at the time, and the book did not immediately become the Jewish Enlightenment's basic text. Almost eighty years passed, in fact, before it was first translated in its entirety into Hebrew, in the new historical context of the Haskalah movement in Russia in the second half of the nineteenth century.

The Haskalah movement—devoted to developing Jewish modernization via innovative schools, journals, a Jewish literature of science, language, geography, and history, and propaganda advocating rectification of the flaws of society— ascribed little importance to Mendelssohn's philosophical discussion of such questions as church-state relations. But it seems that during his lifetime no maskil represented the Jewish Enlightenment in general public opinion as he did. In his time and place, Mendelssohn—the revered symbol of the maskilim who perceived him as a beloved father—was an extraordinary figure. In his dreams, his frustrations, his sensitivity to affront in his public struggles, and his awareness of the responsibility he bore because of his spontaneous designation by Christian public opinion as spokesman of the Jews and representative of Judaism, Mendelssohn was a peerless Jew in his generation. Not one of the other maskilim was as involved as he was in German Enlightenment circles, or was so well known. Because of his unprecedented status Mendelssohn cast a giant shadow over all the other maskilim. David Friedländer, Marcus Herz, and even Wessely were known to the German enlightened who followed cultural developments among the Jews of Berlin, but only Mendelssohn lived in the constant glare of the spotlight of public opinion. No other maskil could pretend to be a successor, a ideological torch-bearer, or a replacement for the man identified by Christians and Jews alike with the Jewish Enlightenment.

8

Specters: The Last Two Years

To MENDELSSOHN's great disappointment *Jerusalem*, his
most important philosophical treatise, did not take Jewish society by storm, and rabbis and maskilim alike paid it scant attention. Of particular concern to Mendelssohn were the quali-
fied, even chilly reactions of the German enlightened. The
ideas in *Jerusalem*, Mendelssohn confessed, are "of such a sort
which neither orthodox nor heterodox people of either nation
expect." In contrast to the praise heaped upon him sixteen years
earlier with the publication of *Phädon*, he now faced increasingly harsh criticism. Still, several notables praised the work; he
particularly prized a letter from Immanuel Kant, who viewed
the book, which presented Judaism as congruent with the principle of freedom of conscience, as a harbinger of great reform.
Kant agreed with Mendelssohn's basic ideas, and further, he
expected them to be the starting point of a process that would
end by stripping Judaism of its historical tenets, annulling its

ritual uniqueness. Kant candidly expressed this in an essay in the 1790s: Why did Mendelssohn not free his brethren from the onerous burden of the religious precepts? Another German philosopher, Johann Gottfried von Herder, who had decisive influence on the change in the cultural climate from rationalist enlightenment to romanticism that nourished national philosophy, also praised the book. But like other critics he actually denied its value, claiming that its political theory was perhaps suited to "a celestial or future Jerusalem" but was not grounded in reality. More caustic and even contemptuous in his negative reaction was Johann Georg Hamann, the radical philosopher from Königsberg, who sought to underscore the power of emotions and faith and undercut the importance ascribed by the Enlightenment to ideas, reason, and philosophy.

Between 1784 and 1785 it became clear to Mendelssohn, to his disappointment, that the philosophical positions and arguments he had put forward in *Jerusalem* had few supporters. The enlightened who inclined toward natural religion could not accept Mendelssohn's adherence to revealed religion and the duty of observing the practical precepts; the orthodox objected to the rejection of the ecclesiastical establishment's ruling power; and the first philosophers of the school later defined as Counter-Enlightenment by the British philosopher Isaiah Berlin attacked *Jerusalem*'s philosophical basis and its belief in reason. Even one of Mendelssohn's closest confidants, the teacher Herz Homberg, who at the time was in Austria, criticized large sections of the book and rejected Mendelssohn's views on the duty of observing the commandments. Mendelssohn, who never labored under delusions, confronted the reality that contradicted his wishes and beliefs. Still, the last two years of his life were tainted by bitter distress at the rejection of the formulae he proposed for the continued existence of the Jews, even in "the modern situation." Mendelssohn's Enlightenment seemed in danger of collapse.

In Mendelssohn's view, the principle of religious tolerance was a sine qua non for the realization of the vision of the Enlightenment in a law-abiding state. But as he realized again and again—first with the mistrustful reactions to his dear friend Lessing's play, *Die Juden*, in the 1750s, then with the traumatic Lavater affair—many intellectuals and politicians still resisted the absolute conclusions required by the general principles of tolerance. The perception of the historical place of the Jews as "other" still prevailed, and civic oppression was the inevitable result. Mendelssohn warned his friends: the barbarism threatening to turn back the clock was lurking everywhere; its targets must vigilantly defend themselves.

In a bitter letter from Vienna at the end of the summer of 1784, Herz Homberg informed Mendelssohn that Homberg's hopes of obtaining a post as a university lecturer had been dashed. Homberg, who had been working for the implementation of Emperor Josef II's toleration laws in the reform of the Jewish education system, had passed all the required examinations, but the emperor would not approve an academic appointment for a Jew. Mendelssohn tried to assuage Homberg's disappointment, but he could not conceal his cynical attitude: "Very infrequently extraordinary people do what ordinary people expect of them, for they are extraordinary people. What His Majesty [the emperor] has decided in your case is therefore not exceptional." Mendelssohn recalled his similar experience, when the Academy of Science had elected him a fellow but the king had not approved the appointment. The insulting blow inflicted upon him by Friedrich II still stung. He had no illusions about absolutist rulers like Friedrich II and Josef II, but all the same he was helpless to explain the incapacity of these two rulers to practice their declared policy of tolerance by recognizing the right of a Jew to become part of the leading scholarly institutions. It was inconceivable, Mendelssohn added wryly, that religious hatred had been the motive behind Homberg's disqualification. He suggested that both friends take what consolation they might in the recognition they had received from the scholars: "Perhaps it is better this way rather than His Majesty approving you, but philosophy would reject you as unworthy."

Mendelssohn's deep suspicions regarding the underlying intentions of Josef II's tolerance policy were manifested in *Jerusalem* in the bitter struggle he portrayed against "the plot of a union of religions." In another letter to Homberg he further stressed his sensitivity toward the warning signs attesting to the problematic nature of Austria's policy:

> Hypocritical toleration seems to me to be more dangerous than open persecution. If I am not mistaken, in his *Persian Letters* Montesquieu poses the destructive notion that it is not rigor and persecution but gentleness and toleration that are best means of conversion. It seems to me that precisely this idea, not wisdom and love of man, that might now be the ruling principle.

In the face of this shrewd threat, he added, there might be a need for the Jews to close ranks, go on the defensive, and entrench themselves behind the Judaism that Mendelssohn described in *Jerusalem*, whose essence was observance of the practical precepts, all in the hope that pluralism might prevail in the future.

In his final days, too, Mendelssohn felt haunted by the demon of anti-Jewish prejudice. In one of his last letters, some two and a half months before his death, he wrote in a tone bordering on despair: "The prejudices against my nation are too deeply rooted as to enable their easy eradication." By the natural course of events, he wrote, even a small part of prejudice left in the soil became the seed of trouble that would soon sprout a new stem. Did the Christians' difficulty in freeing themselves of prejudice, he wondered, call Enlightenment itself into question? In the last two years of his life, in letters to his closest friends, Mendelssohn expressed a fraction of his concerns regarding the failure of the Enlightenment. He was particularly harsh and trenchant in a letter he wrote in September 1784 to the Swiss physician Johann Georg Zimmermann:

> We dreamed of nothing but the Enlightenment and believed that the light of reason would illumine all around it with such power that delusion and inflamed fanaticism would no longer be able to be seen. But as we can see, from beyond the horizon the night rises once more with all its specters. Most frightening of all is that evil is so active and influential. Delusion and enthusiasm [*Schwärmerey*] act, and reason makes do with words.

What did Mendelssohn mean by these words? What were the ghosts that troubled his peace of mind at night? First was the heavy hand of establishment religion, which threatened to stifle religious tolerance. For Mendelssohn, continued civic oppression and discrimination and the failure to uproot Christian prejudice against the Jews were the most worrying symptoms. He was no less troubled and surprised by the awakening of the Romantic trend in literature, the theater, and German philosophy. In the early 1770s arose the cultural revolution that brought the romantic movement of Sturm und Drang (storm and stress). This dynamic outburst aimed to upend the Enlightenment's philosophy of reason and replace it with naturalness, emotion, subjectivity, and spontaneity. Like some of his close colleagues, Mendelssohn was revolted by this phenomenon and feared that its suppression of reason would bring back superstition in a new guise. So Mendelssohn spent the last two years of his life in a dark world filled on the one hand with religious fanaticism unrestrained by reason (*Aberglaube*, overbelief), on the other hand bereft of the presence of God (heresy). The life of a man without belief in God, Mendelssohn wrote in 1784 in a dedication of one of his portraits, is not life but a slow death. The existence of God in the world was the basis of all the humanistic principles Mendelssohn believed in. Without God, man could not exist.

How, then, could he exorcise these evil spirits that were destroying the very structure of the Enlightenment? In a short article he published in the *Berlinische Monatsschrift* in the winter of 1785, Mendelssohn laid the blame for the outbreak of these two evils—lack of belief and overbelief—at least partially on the Enlightenment itself. The radical Enlightenment of Voltaire—employing as he had the tactics of harsh, acerbic satire against religious fervor and superstition—had, Mendelssohn was convinced, acted as a boomerang. Not only was denigration inappropriate for cultivating the Enlightenment, but it inspired in some people a contrary yearning to return to childish innocence, to live in a fairytale world rather than live without God. In Mendelssohn's opinion, so long as German culture was dominated by the rationalistic philosophy of Leibniz and Wolff, with its clear concepts and firm arguments, religious fervor and atheism based on superficial concepts were powerless. Instead of what he viewed as the sham and negative French Enlightenment, Mendelssohn proposed the path of the true and positive Enlightenment: "The source of this evil can be stopped up only by means of the Enlightenment. Illuminate the environment and the specters will vanish. . . . The vocation of Man is not the suppression of prejudice but its illumination." In a widely discussed short article, *Über die Frage: was heißt Aufklären?* (On the question: What is enlightenment?), published in 1784, Mendelssohn wrote more systematically on the limits and dangers of enlightenment. The context of this article was a prolonged critical debate at the Berlin Wednesday Society on a subject that the intellectuals committed to Enlightenment values would have found surprising. It can be framed simply in the question: is it appropriate to constrain the Enlightenment so that the state and society will not be harmed? Mendelssohn, a respected member of the group of intellectuals who regularly attended these meetings, took an active part in the debate. At first he raised several points for discussion by the members, and in September 1784 his article was published in the society's *Berlinische Monatsschrift*. At the end of the year the monthly published a response from Immanuel Kant, *Beantwortung der Frage: Was ist Aufklärung?* (Answering the question: What is enlightenment?) in which he set out his celebrated definition that equates enlightenment with the liberation of the autonomous and thinking man from the shackles of authority, and thus with modernization itself:

> Enlightenment is man's release from his self-incurred tutelage. Tutelage is man's inability to make use of his understanding without direction from another. Self-incurred is this tutelage when its cause lies not in lack of reason but in lack of resolution and courage to use it without direction from another. Sapere aude! "Have courage to use your own reason!"—that is the motto of enlightenment.

Answering the concern that enlightenment is potentially politically subversive, Kant noted that only freedom of thought is unrestricted and that obedience to government and law is an undeniable duty. Mendelssohn had underscored the problematic side of enlightenment, especially the tension between enlightenment—which he defined as "reasoned recognition and skillful thinking on matters pertaining to the life of man"—and the state. He pointed to the possible confrontation between man as man and man as a citizen of the state, as well as the possible contradiction between the good of society and scientific and philosophical advances. Less than five years before the French Revolution, Mendelssohn considered whether unlimited freedom and unrestricted critical enlightenment might harm the public and bring about dangerous revolutions. What, he wondered, was the thin line between the amelioration of social life and its destruction? And what was the balance between the struggle against prejudice and the stability of society? Mendelssohn also raised a particularly interesting point regarding the achievements of modern science and their influence on society. Like many others in Europe who were profoundly impressed by the hot-air balloon invented by the Montgolfier brothers in France in 1783, Mendelssohn raised one of the modernist's most incisive critical questions: "The discovery by the Montgolfier brothers will probably lead to great revolutions. Whether they will be for the good of human society nobody will as yet dare to decide. But who will on this account hesitate to promote progress? The discovery of eternal truths is as such good; it is for Providence to take care of them in the right direction." In his essay Mendelssohn identified two conditions he considered insufferable, under which the Enlightenment seemed doomed to failure. In his view the philosophical, conceptual, and ideological debate over the definition and characteristics of the Enlightenment was not abstract but was connected with man's accomplishing both his essential vocation as a being discrete in its intelligent cognition from the rest of the world's creatures and his vocation as a citizen of the state. "Without the essential vocations of man qua man he sinks to the level of the beast," Mendelssohn stressed, "and without the essential vocations of the citizen, governance in the state cannot exist." The Enlightenment would fail, on the one hand, if it were perceived by leaders of the state as a threat to the regime, which would thus deny Enlightenment to its citizens. On the other hand, the Enlightenment would fail if its radical representatives misused it with the aim of destroying religion and morality. In both of these confrontational conditions Mendelssohn proposed that the Enlightenment must be restricted because the damage in its dissemination and promotion would be greater than the benefits. Latent in the description of the first condition is Mendelssohn's bitter criticism of the Prussian state that oppressed the Jews, as he himself had experienced. In his opinion, the Enlightenment of a nation is determined by its dissemination among all classes. As he saw it, bringing man's Enlightenment and civil class into opposition creates a tragic situation:

> Woe betide the country that is compelled to admit to itself that the essential vocation of Man and the essential vocation of the citizen in it are incongruent; that Enlightenment, which is a necessity for humankind, cannot spread in it to all classes without threatening the existence of the regime. Here it must be said to philosophy: keep quiet! Here the need to dictate laws is likely, or more precisely, to strengthen the shackles that must be put on humankind to subjugate it and leave it under a perpetual yoke!

Revealed again in his description of the second condition for failure are his abhorrence of radical Enlightenment and his fear of the specters of heresy:

> If it is not possible to disseminate a certain and elevated truth that is beneficial to man without completely destroying the principles of religion and morality dwelling within it at the time, then it is incumbent upon the disseminator of Enlightenment, to which the beneficent state is dear, to act circumspectly and moderately. And it would be better for him to suffer prejudice rather than drive out, together with it, its inherent truth without separating them.

According to Mendelssohn, this is the price that the truly enlightened must pay out of their responsibility to the stability of society. "Abuse of Enlightenment," Mendelssohn cautioned his colleagues in the Enlightenment community toward the end of this article, "weakens the moral sense and spawns stiff-neckedness, egotism, heresy, and anarchy."

Even as Mendelssohn persevered desperately to defend what he perceived as the true Enlightenment against those who threatened it on various fronts, in his last years his physical condition deteriorated. His illness, which had never completely disappeared, continued to cause him great suffering, severely limiting his activities. On more than one occasion he apologized for being unable to attend one of the numerous social events to which he was invited. The evenings were hardest for him. He did his best to avoid any excitement, and only in the morning hours did he enjoy relative relief and the chance to indulge in intellectual activity. But not all in his life was gloomy, and he enjoyed moments of satisfaction and happiness. On the morning of September 6, 1785, Mendelssohn's closest friends came to his home for a surprise celebration of his fifty-sixth birthday—sadly, his last. That morning he felt wonderful. The pain eased for a while, and his spirits were more buoyant than ever. A better company, he wrote to Herz Homberg immediately after the party, could not be found in all of Germany. In this small circle, surrounded by true friends committed to the Enlightenment cause, he felt protected, liked, even loved. "I am alive," Mendelssohn declared to Homberg in an outburst of rejuvenated vitality and with plans for new works in his mind, "and I hope to prove this to you by the time of the forthcoming fair, when you shall read my little book *Über das Daseyn Gottes* (On the existence of God)."

During those two years his family, too, gave him great joy. On doctor's orders the family took a stroll along Berlin's boulevards almost every day. Mendelssohn had a special love for his youngest son, Nathan, who was only three, and playing with the child helped him forget his distress for a short while. Fromet continued in her role as hostess of the open salon of the Mendelssohn home, serving tea, almonds, and raisins to the guests, and occasionally participating in the conversation. A letter Mendelssohn wrote in 1773—to a young Catholic medical student from Köln who sought justification for sex before marriage—affords us an extraordinary look into his personal world. Evident in his reply is the importance he attributes to love between husband and wife, as well as his conception of the nature of married life. Mendelssohn draws a distinction between base sensual desire, whose gratification is sinful, and the passion of natural love, whose aim, according to the laws of nature, is the shared conception of a human being. The man is duty bound to protect the woman during her pregnancy, Mendelssohn wrote, and with her provide for all of their offspring's needs. Man and wife share responsibility for raising their child, he emphasized, and the best way of enforcing that responsibility is by means of a legally binding marriage contract. And indeed, Moses and Fromet Mendelssohn invested great effort in raising and educating their children, trying to ensure a happy childhood for them. Mendelssohn boasted to his friends that his sons and daughters excelled in their studies with the help of private tutors who taught them every day, and that they were being educated as enlightened youngsters. Living standards in the Mendelssohn home had risen with the family's ascent of the social ladder. The childhood friends of Brendel, Reikel, Joseph, Jente, and Abraham were numbered among Berlin's Jewish aristocracy. They enjoyed summer vacations together, attended the theater and concerts, and read German and French literature.

The marriages of the two eldest girls, Brendel and Reikel, exemplified this bourgeois milieu of an upper-class Berlin Jewish family whose lifestyle combined the traditional and the modern. Both were married in Mendelssohn's last years, and in no small part at his initiative, in accordance with the accepted marriage practices of traditional Judaism: through a match made at an early age and in a traditional ceremony. At age eighteen Brendel married Simon Veit, a young banker of whom Mendelssohn was very fond; Reikel married Mendel Meyer, the son of Nathan Meyer, court factor in the Duchy of Mecklenburg-Strelitz, when she was seventeen. Mendelssohn was convinced that with these good marriages he was ensuring his daughters' happiness. He joyfully wrote to Brendel's former tutor Homberg of her marriage: "with the peerless Veit she is living a happy married life."

Brendel was married to Veit for sixteen years and had four children, two of whom died, but a more accurate portrayal of her happiness is provided by a close friend of her youth, Henriette Herz, wife of the philosopher Marcus Herz and a popular hostess in Berlin's haut monde. Herz wrote in her memoirs of meeting Brendel Mendelssohn-Veit after her marriage and finding her far from happy. Although her father had not forced Brendel to marry Veit, Herz complained, nor had he bothered to consult her. According to her friend, the marriage cut short Brendel's youth and made her miserable. It was inconceivable to Herz that a young girl like Brendel who had received a broad and enlightened education would fall in love with a merchant who was not handsome, who was narrow-minded, and whose standing as a man of culture was lower than her own.

Brendel's unsatisfactory and joyless marriage came to an end in the late 1790s, but in the earlier words of Henriette Herz we can hear the reverberations of the new era in the Berlin community, an era that Mendelssohn could hardly even imagine. In contrast with the Mendelssohn home, which strictly maintained life according to religious law, the traditional customs, Sabbaths, and festivals, and Jewish education for boys and girls, life was different in other homes of Berlin's Jewish elite. Over the years fewer of the younger generation remained loyal to the synagogue, to observance of the precepts. Mendelssohn was aware that these processes were eroding the Jewish identity he had nurtured, but he was characteristically tolerant. Perhaps he hoped by means of the written word—his own judicious and incisive arguments against heresy and his reasoning in favor of the duty of observance of the commandments—to slow these trends.

Mendelssohn had been aware of Brendel's unstable character and her constant dissatisfaction since her childhood, but he was unprepared for her extramarital affair with the writer Friedrich Schlegel, her divorce, her conversion to Christianity, and her subsequent marriage to Schlegel. Two grandchildren, whom he never saw, grew up to become the noted Christian artists Johannes and Philipp Veit. Mendelssohn's son Joseph, who he dreamed would be his heir and successor, also tested the philosopher's tolerance toward the trends that ran counter to his worldview. Joseph, Mendelssohn told Herz Homberg, stopped learning Hebrew and had almost forgotten everything his father had taught him. But Mendelssohn resolved not to force unwanted lessons on his son, for that would violate his philosophical objection to coercion.

The family idyll that Mendelssohn believed in continued to sustain him. "My wife, my son-in-law, my daughter, and son are all good and enlightened people (*aufklärungswürdige Menschen*)," he wrote with unconcealed pride to Johann Zimmermann in the summer of 1784. A particularly elating experience for him was studying with three young students. His son Joseph, his new son-in-law Simon Veit, and Bernhard Wessely, a friend of the family, all in their teens and thirsty for knowledge, rose early for these sessions. In those early-morning hours Mendelssohn's mind was clear and his illness did not trouble him. Through conversation, debate, and sometimes a disciplined lecture, Mendelssohn sought to keep the younger generation from what he perceived as one of the greatest dangers: loss of faith in God. He did not present them with the commandments of the Jewish religion, did not speak of divine revelation, did not analyze religious texts, but as he had done in his proof of the immortality of the soul, he appealed instead to philosophy and provided his pupils with a series of rational proofs. According to his philosophy, the existence of God was the loftiest of the "eternal truths" that every man is capable of achieving through the virtue of reason, and therefore their discussion was not based on Jewish religious creed. This study in the quiet, invigorating morning hours gave birth to one of Mendelssohn's most important treatises, *Morgenstunden oder Vorlesungen über das Daseyn Gottes* (Morning hours; or, Lectures on the existence of God), printed at the end of the summer of 1785. "Morning Hours" is Mendelssohn's apologia on behalf of his friend Lessing, and it was further inspired by his distress and frustration over the *Pantheismusstreit* (the strife over pantheism), a controversy linking his friend with Spinoza's ideas. Similar to the "Letter to Deacon Lavater" of 1770 and *Jerusalem* of 1783, "Morning Hours" was a counterargument. This time his adversary was a sophisticated and opinionated philosopher, a serious critic of the Berlin Enlightenment in its entirety, whom Mendelssohn had never met face to face: Friedrich Heinrich Jacobi of Düsseldorf.

Lessing, who had died in 1781, continued to occupy a central place in Mendelssohn's world. Not only had their friendship left an ineradicable mark on him, their closeness was a cornerstone of his status in German public opinion. In Mendelssohn's salon was a bust of Lessing standing beneath the portraits of Greek philosophers and the leader of the scientific revolution, Isaac Newton. Following the publication of *Jerusalem* Mendelssohn informed his friends that he intended to write a treatise on Lessing and thus repay his great debt to his friend. Nothing prepared him for the fact that this plan, which never came to fruition, would develop into a harsh and stormy affair that would engage scholars during the last two years of his life and whose repercussions would continue after his death.

Friedrich Jacobi learned of Mendelssohn's plan to write the book in a letter written to him by Elise Reimarus of Hamburg, whom Mendelssohn had met at Bad Pyrmont. Reimarus, an educated woman and one of Mendelssohn's admirers and correspondents, had known Lessing in her youth. Jacobi decided to exploit this acquaintance to strike a blow at the Berlin

Enlightenment. In the 1780s he and Hamann, his friend from Königsberg, represented the unexpected trend of counter-Enlightenment. These spokesmen accused the enlightened of heresy while criticizing philosophical rationalism. In their opinion only religious faith could consolidate recognition of God since the truth could not be attained through philosophy. They also rejected the "Berlin mentality" as arrogant and authoritarian. Hamann even wrote a book targeting Mendelssohn's *Jerusalem* and accusing him of nothing less than atheism. In his view, Mendelssohn was part of the secular subversive, materialistic, and anti-Christian group embodied in Berlin, the "Modern Babylon."

Through Elise Reimarus's innocuous mediation, Jacobi disseminated on the Enlightenment correspondence network the shocking revelation that Lessing, the hero of the Berlin Enlightenment, had in fact been an atheist. The principal addressee of this accusation was Mendelssohn, and Jacobi awaited his response to this sensational news. In private conversations in Lessing's last years, Jacobi related, he had admitted to having become a Spinozist. The identification of anyone with the doctrine of the seventeenth-century Dutch-Jewish philosopher Baruch Spinoza could mean only one thing: denial of the existence of God. Spinozism was a denigrating name in German culture, the majority of whose philosophers were at the outside deists, who believed in natural religion (the existence of God, divine providence, the immortality of the soul); only a few—materialists, for instance, who believed only in the existence of tangible material—denied the existence of God. Spinoza's pantheism, which was understood as total unity between the world and God (as Mendelssohn put it: all is one and one is all) and denial of the existence of God discrete from nature, was perceived as heresy, and Spinoza was notorious as an enemy of religion. For Spinoza, Jacobi contended, nature had become God.

From Mendelssohn's standpoint, Jacobi's exposure of Lessing—the veracity of which he did not doubt; he was tormented only by the question of how to explain it—bore numerous dire implications, some very personal and others touching upon the very nature of his worldview: had his close friend Lessing concealed his true views from him and revealed them to another whom he trusted more? Was this not testimony that the friendship he had held so dear was not as strong as he thought? Must he attempt to refute this accusation and clear Lessing's name? Did Lessing's exposure as a devotee of Spinoza's doctrine besmirch Mendelssohn, too, as a possible heretic? Was he obliged now to cross swords with Spinoza's philosophical theory? And was it to be he who would represent the "true" Enlightenment and defend rationalistic philosophy against its counter-Enlightenment adversaries who sided with "blind faith"? At first Mendelssohn tried to make light of the rumors or to interpret them more moderately. He thought he could avoid confrontation with the excuse of weakness and prolonged illness, but ultimately he found himself, as he had in previous affairs, compelled to fight back and to defend his world, and particularly his confidence in the power of reason to consolidate recognition of God and his loyalty to Lessing.

Mendelssohn could not help but discern anti-Jewish overtones in the words of Hamann and Jacobi. The "Berlin mentality" they so abhorred was presented as showing a Jewish influence. Mendelssohn's centrality in Enlightenment circles was evidence of the justness of their words, as was the fact that Spinoza, too, the father of philosophical heresy, was himself a Jew. If that were not enough, another tract published at the end of 1784 by Johann Schulz attacked Mendelssohn for his criticism of atheism in *Jerusalem* as endangering the morals of society, when Judaism itself, Schulz insisted, was the source of all fanaticism and intolerance. Isaac Euchel, who visited Mendelssohn at his home at the time, heard from him a somewhat cynical remark that illustrated his feeling of being trapped: he was like the husband, he told Euchel, whose wife accuses him of impotence while the maidservant accuses him of causing her pregnancy.

Mendelssohn's confidants testified to his great agitation and the emotional stress he was under. He decided to postpone writing his treatise on Lessing, concentrating instead on the clash with Jacobi. Initially the confrontation had been conducted in private correspondence, but in the course of 1781 it was revealed to the general public. Mendelssohn's defense of Lessing was included in "Morning Hours," which identified two enemies of the Enlightenment's rationalistic philosophy who held diametrically opposed attitudes toward God: the materialists, who denied the possibility of the existence of an invisible entity, and the enthusiastic mystics, including the kabbalists, who by means of extreme piety sought to attain a direct encounter with God. The distance between superstition and the delusions of religious fanatics and the deniers of the existence of God, Mendelssohn asserted, is in fact very short. Philosophy is the only appropriate weapon in the war against these specters. Skepticism and reasoning defend truth against prejudice. Even Spinoza's method is worthy of deeper examination, after which it can be refined and mounted on steadier legs that leave room for the existence of God. In Mendelssohn's view, Lessing subscribed to Spinoza's pure approach, as he interpreted it in "Morning Hours": a world exists beyond God but is dependent on the existence of God. Therefore man is not a slave to a natural reality over which he has no control, but in accordance with humanistic belief he is a free creature and responsible for his actions, and like all Creation is dependent upon God but also maintains his independent existence and value as a human being.

The affair reached its climax when Jacobi, in his tract *Über die Lehre des Spinoza in Briefen an Herrn Moses Mendelssohn* (Concerning the doctrine of Spinoza in letters to Mr. Moses Mendelssohn), revealed publicly the confrontation between him and Mendelssohn and its source, Lessing's sensational confession. In this tract Jacobi reiterated his claim that Spinoza's radical rationalistic doctrine is heresy, denounced Enlightenment philosophy in general and Lessing in particular, and fired barbs at Mendelssohn. Mendelssohn's sense of injury was exacerbated by the appearance in the book of the specter that had haunted him for more than a decade—in his tract Jacobi quoted Lavater, the first to attack Mendelssohn with missionary zeal, to bolster his criticism of rationalistic philosophy and his arguments regarding the preeminence of pure belief.

The last three months of Mendelssohn's life stood in the bleak shadow of this affair. Although his social life remained active and he continued to receive visitors and reply to correspondence, he was preoccupied with the task of clearing Lessing's name. In a letter, charged with affront, to Immanuel Kant, he asked how Jacobi could have done a deed so despicable from the points of view both of public morality and of the accepted rules of behavior in scholarly circles:

> How could Jacobi have betrayed the secret of his departed friend and reveal it not only to me, from whom he [Lessing] had carefully concealed it, but to the whole world? He saves his own skin and leaves his friend naked and defenseless in an open field to become the prey of and object of derision by his enemies. I cannot accept such behavior and I would like to know what honest men like you think of it. I fear that philosophy has its fanatics who like religious fanatics persecute others with great force and are even more inclined toward conversion than they.

At the same time Mendelssohn became increasingly suspicious—or perhaps obsessive—that this was not simply philosophical fanaticism. He and the Berlin publisher Nicolai, his loyal friend for years, concluded that the Jacobi affair was a distasteful plot to pressure him to convert. In their view, "the Lavater clique," driven by Christian missionary zeal, sought to defame Mendelssohn as a heretic. Thus they would demonstrate the slippery slope between rationalistic philosophy and skepticism and loss of faith, all to save the Christian "banner of faith" from the threat of the Enlightenment.

In the winter of 1785 Mendelssohn, assailed by a storm of emotion, wrote his response to Jacobi—the last piece he wrote—*An die Freunde Lessings* (To Lessing's friends). In this tract, which he did not live to see in print, he demonstrated how, in his opinion, Jacobi had maneuvered Lessing into a trap to make it appear that the latter subscribed to Spinoza's doctrine and pantheism so that Jacobi could suggest the only escape route from all metaphysical snares: the truth would be found only in religious belief. Having accumulated much experience in several similar affairs, Mendelssohn wrote, he had suspected Jacobi's hidden intentions from the outset. But as the previous attempts at converting him had failed, he continued, so would this cleverer one. And here, as if he knew that these were his final days, he reiterated the main principles of his belief as they had been developed two years earlier in *Jerusalem:* "I, therefore, do not believe that the resources of human reason are inadequate to the persuading of mankind of the eternal truths requisite for their happiness." Only the revelation of divine revelation on Mount Sinai, on which religious authority is based, is a matter of faith, he declared, but revelation or faith are not, according to the principles of Judaism, appropriate ways of knowing of the existence and providence of God. "Judaism," Mendelssohn reiterated his credo, "is not a *revealed religion* (*geoffenbarte Religion*) but a *revealed law* (*geoffenbartes Gesetz*)." Nothing would shake his belief in the power of reason, and nothing would move him from adhering to the religion of his forefathers.

Mendelssohn wrote these words almost as a last will and testament; they were the concluding lines of the role he had played for thirty years on the stage of the German republic of letters, the ones by which he wished to be remembered in public opinion. He wrote impatiently, conscious of the dwindling sand in the hourglass of his life. He wanted to see "To Lessing's Friends" printed as expeditiously as possible in order to hasten his repudiation of Jacobi's hurtful claims. He wrote its concluding sentences on Friday, December 30, 1785. At the end of the Sabbath the following evening, only a few hours before the end of 1785, he left his house in haste to hand over the manuscript to the publisher Christian Friedrich Voss. On his return home he felt relieved that the distressing affair was over.

His wife, solicitous of his failing health, had begged him not to hurry so, Fromet Mendelssohn told the people who came to her home to console her, at least to put on a warm coat to protect him against the December cold of Berlin's streets, but he would not listen. After the visit to the publisher, Mendelssohn fell ill with a cold, and his condition deteriorated rapidly. No one in the family and his circle of friends imagined that these were his final hours. On Monday, Dr. Marcus Herz, called to attend him, diagnosed a cough and weakness, but no ailment serious enough to require treatment. The cough worsened the next day, the chest pain intensified, and Dr. Markus Bloch joined Herz in an attempt to ease his suffering. Dr. Herz told about his last visit and Mendelssohn's last words: "I found him lying in his bed in a fur coat and he looked very bad, and he told me, My illness is very grievous today, I cannot rid myself of the phlegm on my chest, I cannot eat, I cannot sleep and all my strength is spent." On the morning of Wednesday, January 4, 1786, after an exhausting and sleepless night, Moses Mendelssohn died. Marcus Herz's medical report on Mendelssohn's illness and death, which was published three weeks later in the preface to "To Lessing's Friends," concludes dramatically:

I heard a sound from the couch [where Mendelssohn lay]. I ran back into the room and there he lay . . . his head thrown back, foam on his lips. Signs of respiration, a pulse, of life, had ceased. We attempted to resuscitate him in a number of ways, but in vain. He lay there . . . on his lips his familiar cordial smile, as if an angel had taken him from this earth with a kiss. . . . The light in room went out as the oil in the lamp was finished. . . . In that first terrible moment I immediately clutched his head and remained petrified in that position for God knows how long. I wanted to fall down at his side and die with him.

There is no way of knowing how Mendelssohn's life would have turned out had he heeded his wife's advice and stayed home on that cold night rather than rushing his response to Jacobi to the printer. His close friends who mourned his passing viewed the *Pantheismusstreit* as the affair that shortened his life, since it had put him under such great stress that his already weakened body failed him. Some went so far as to claim that Mendelssohn had been maliciously, cold-bloodedly, and mercilessly murdered by Jacobi. One of them, the writer Karl Philipp Moritz, published this explicit accusation three weeks after Mendelssohn's death: "[Mendelssohn] was a victim of his friendship with Lessing and died a martyr's death defending the trampled rights of reason against fanaticism and superstition. Lavater dealt his life the first blow. Jacobi completed the work." These harsh words accorded Mendelssohn's death heroic dimensions and bolstered his image. In the eyes of his admirers he was depicted as a martyr of the Enlightenment who gave his life for its principles, and as a victim of the plot laid against him by his enemies.

The myth of Mendelssohn as the hero of the German and Jewish Enlightenment grew after his death. But the milieu in which he had been active changed rapidly after his death. The social and cultural trends developed in new directions, few of which he could have predicted in his last years. Toward the end of the eighteenth century the counter-Enlightenment and Romanticism gathered momentum in German culture. Anti-Enlightenment reaction also reinforced reservations about ending Jewish civil oppression, and during the nineteenth century it nourished modern anti-Semitism. In contrast, the French Revolution, which took place three and a half years after Mendelssohn's death, shook the conventions and basic vales of cultural and political order in Europe but also created the first precedent of parliamentary legislation granting political rights to Jews.

In Berlin's Jewish society in general and the Mendelssohn family in particular, the cultural and social amalgamation with the German bourgeoisie accelerated. Many young Jews considered Judaism irrelevant to life in a European metropolis. Four of Moses and Fromet Mendelssohn's children—Brendel, Jente, Abraham, and Joseph—eventually converted to Christianity, embracing social acculturation and its many advantages, including the possibility of marrying non-Jews. Considering the stubborn battles Mendelssohn had fought against those who would save his soul by persuading him to convert, his children's turn to Christianity is an historic irony. The Jewish Enlightenment and the enterprise of establishing a new Jewish library continued for another decade after Mendelssohn's death, until its leading figures concluded that the alternative Jewish culture they proposed had little to offer the majority of the sons and daughters of Berlin's Jewish elite.

It therefore seems that unlike the mythical Mendelssohn, the historic Mendelssohn cannot be separated from his time and generation. Instead of judging him as the man responsible for the processes of change, integration, assimilation, breakdown, reform, and renewal undergone by European Jewish society in the succeeding generations, instead of trapping him in the image and myth of a Jewish-German hero, we must attempt to understand the meaning of the story of his life as a famous Berlin Jew in the thirty years between the mid-1750s and the 1780s. Mendelssohn's fame was one of the most fascinating historical events in the early stages of the Jews' modern era. His entry into the public arena—by virtue of his intellectual talents and his full partnership in the shaping of German Enlightenment culture through his ideas, books, articles, conversations, and social contacts—made a Jew, for the first time, a well-known and admired public figure. It is not surprising that the question arose whether the "Mendelssohn event" mandated rethinking the attitude of culture, the Christian religion, and the state toward the Jews and Judaism. Did the "Mendelssohn event" mean that the barriers between Jews and non-Jews would fall? Would Mendelssohn, like the biblical Moses, lead his people toward a new phase in their history? Mendelssohn himself quickly realized that he had become a sensation and that his fame was the result of his success as a philosopher. Many people read his work, listened to his words, visited his home, invited him to theirs, and corresponded with him. Although on numerous occasions he expressed his wish to remain in his study, it seems that he and his family generally enjoyed the public exposure, the honor heaped upon him, and the friends and admirers who sought their company in high society. He viewed every word written about him as important, and by means of an intricate web of correspondence he followed the responses to and critiques of his publications. His visits to the courts of princes and the direct encounters with the haut monde in his salon or at Bad Pyrmont gave him great satisfaction.

But this fame came with a price. Now and again he was asked by his Jewish brethren to act as their representative and on occasion as their mediator and lobbyist, and as the most famous Jew of his generation, he was perceived as a leader of the Jews and the instantly recognizable representative of Judaism. This was a role that Mendelssohn accepted reluctantly. Now and again, as in his defense of distressed Jewish communities, or his initiative that led to Dohm's treatise, he undoubtedly felt that he was able to exploit his status beneficially and function as a political leader of sorts. Fame and status also compelled him to enter public debates and repel, over and over, the claim that commitment to both Judaism and the Enlightenment was contradictory. At the same time such forums gave him an opportunity to preach humanism and present his perception of the Enlightenment to an attentive audience.

Despite Mendelssohn's fame, social success, and deep involvement in European literature and philosophy, he and his family continued to maintain the lifestyle of typical Berlin Jews: they maintained traditional patterns, including active membership in the community's leadership and synagogue, and observance of the practical precepts, the Sabbath, festivals, and the dietary laws. From the perspective of the intellectual world of the Jews of his generation, Mendelssohn was a typical representative of a new phenomenon—the early Enlightenment. The foundations of his culture were religious, and it was reasonable to assume that he would go on to pursue a rabbinical career. A tempestuous attraction toward philosophy motivated him, like many others of the early Enlightenment, to contribute to strengthening the rationalistic foundations of Judaism (relying in great measure on the cultural precedents of medieval Judaism and the intellectuals' preferred representative of that Judaism—Maimonides), to demand renewed and in-depth study of the Bible, and to break out of the closed Jewish house of study and examine such values as aesthetics, humanism, and broad knowledge of man and his natural environment. Even though *Jerusalem*, his most important work, was not written exclusively for a Jewish readership, it included a proposed solution to ensure the Jews' continued existence under modern conditions. According to Mendelssohn's liberal dream, the state would become increasingly tolerant, and the civil govornment and the churches would not be interdependent in the future. The prejudices of Christianity would no longer provide a basis for oppression of the Jews. According to Mendelssohn, the Jews would continue to maintain their national integrity, but their membership in the communities would be voluntary, and they would observe the commandments out of inner persuasion, without the rabbis' coercive threat of punishment.

Although the two men never met face to face, the shadow of King Friedrich II of Prussia hung over Mendelssohn's life. The hostile signals Mendelssohn received from the king—especially the humiliating rejection of his 1771 election to the Royal Academy of Science—symbolized the specter of civic oppression. Quite a few of his bitter turns of phrase against discrimination and the forces that fed anti-Jewish prejudice even in the times of Enlightenment were trenchantly subversive, if circumspectly worded, criticisms of this monarch. Mendelssohn was sent contradictory messages from the milieu in which he lived and worked. On the one hand, honors were lavished upon him and he was admired as the "German Socrates," while on the other he felt he was being conspired against, that his adversaries were laying in wait for him to abandon his Jewish origins. Frustrating tensions roiled his intellectual life, and his mood fluctuated between dreams of the triumph of humanistic values and nightmares of the distortion of the Enlightenment and denial of reason and liberty. He believed wholeheartedly that the state would become pluralistic, fully internalize the value of tolerance, and allow all men to attain happiness free of coercion, but again and again he was oppressed by the understanding that it would not come about in the foreseeable future and that humankind would not easily adapt to what seemed so right, just, and obvious.

Thus his life was defined in part by the tension between his Jewish identity as the "other" and his prominent public status. More than once this "otherness" left him feeling helpless and weak, affronted and vulnerable. One such moment was on that stroll down Unter den Linden, when youths threw stones at him and his family. His feelings were similar when he read Michaelis's criticism of Lessing's *Die Juden*, when he was stunned by Lavater's and Cranz's challenge, and when he was attacked by Jacobi. But Mendelssohn's sense of "otherness" as a Jew did not mean only that he was an eternal victim exposed to attack; it also provided him with a singular point of view. As a leading player in German Enlightenment circles and as a Jew, he was able to observe his surroundings from two viewpoints, as both a partner from within and a critic from without. Mendelssohn, more than others, was able to assess the limits of the Enlightenment, as he did, for instance, in "On the Question: What Is Enlightenment?" The otherness forced upon him as a Jew enabled him to examine the borderlines around him from the perspective of civil inferiority and discrimination, and that experience made him immune to being swept away on the belief that modern European culture would necessarily bring happiness to people, that it made inevitable the march of human progress. He felt elated when he heard of Emperor Josef II's Edicts of Tolerance, when he read Lessing's *Nathan der Weise* and Dohm's *Über die bürgerliche Verbesserung der Juden*, but he always had reservations and displayed circumspection. He always asked whether a step would lead toward toleration, and whether the intentions underlying it were pure.

Although Mendelssohn was a disciple of the optimistic philosophy of Leibniz, his natural skepticism, fed by his acute awareness of his situation as a Jew, made it difficult for him to naïvely accept Leibniz's basic concept that this world is the best of all possible worlds. Mendelssohn knew that some frontiers were still closed to him by deeply rooted prejudices, and that negative stereotypes of the Jews created obstacles even for his Enlightenment colleagues. When he suspected, during a period of enthusiasm over Josef II's tolerance policy, that the modern state sought to make the Jews' surrender of their religious uniqueness a condition of their right to "civil happiness," he interpreted the restriction as a grave perversion of the principle of tolerance and declared that it would be better for the Jews to remain without rights. His caution suggests a belief that tyrannical and ruthless trends might develop from Enlightenment itself—like the frightening notion of a "union of religions." He also abhorred the extreme anticlerical stand of the French Enlightenment, which would, he feared, shake the very foundations of cultural order and human morality.

The story of Mendelssohn's life and works reveals him as the first real Jewish humanist. Although Spinoza had called for religious tolerance and freedom of thought and expression, from the perspective of Jewish society his philosophical endeavor was identified mainly as criticism of the Jewish religion. Nor did Spinoza, situated as he was on the margins of the Jewish community of his time, face the challenges engaged by Mendelssohn, who was immersed in the "modern situation" of the Jews. No Jewish philosopher before Mendelssohn had to negotiate such dilemmas of Jewish existence as those that had emerged and continued to emerge in the changing European society of Mendelssohn's time, and none so fully embraced, as a principle of the highest order, concern for human dignity and the rights to freedom and happiness. All his philosophical ideas, including his view of Judaism as a religion averse to coercion and proselytization of faith, derived from his humanism—as did the struggles he endured. Mendelssohn's Man is the loftiest creature created by God. His qualities as a thinking, observing, and feeling creature possessing an immortal soul motivate him to rise above his physical limitations and base instincts and aspire toward perfection.

Mendelssohn's existence as a Jew heightened his sensitivity to wrongdoing, oppression, cruelty, and injustice. He was revolted by the horrors of war and the destruction it sows; he described public executions in shocking terms; he condemned suicide; he sought to weaken the power of the state and its hold over the lives of its citizens; he fought against religious coercion; he protested vigorously against the excommunication and ostracism meted out by priests and rabbis, and repeatedly spoke out against religious fanaticism, torture, acts of barbarism, banishment, and discrimination. His Enlightenment was humanistic, and in every philosophical debate in which he took part he examined its implications for man. He grounded his hopes for the end to restrictions imposed upon the Jews on the humanistic ethos in which he believed. Like his friend Lessing in *Nathan der Weise*, Mendelssohn viewed the recognition that the Jew is a human being as the basis for any change of attitude toward the Jews. His reasoned recognition of God was the basis upon which he grounded his humanistic values. Throughout his life he abhorred heresy and invested great intellectual effort in proving that God can be recognized by means of the reason with which every human being is blessed. Without the existence of a merciful God who seeks the good and perfection of human beings, he declared, the humanistic concept collapses. Mendelssohn believed that man as conceived by the materialists—simply a biological and physiological machine—left no room for values and justice, no purpose to life, no point in man's aspirations to learn and improve himself, and no basis for nurturing virtues and morality. Mendelssohn's God, however, is not the exclusive God of the Jews but the God of all humankind. Although he believed in the tradition of the divine revelation to the Jews on Mount Sinai, and in the special obligations deriving from that revelation to observe the laws and preserve the historical heritage and national Jewish life, he held God to be a Creator who seeks the success and good of all his creatures. By means of their intelligence, Mendelssohn believed, human beings could recognize God without need of revelation, sacred books, or the guidance of any particular church.

Contrary to the myths associated with him, Mendelssohn was not the historic figure who should be credited with the changes that dramatically altered the face of the Jewish people in the modern era. He was not the leader of a modernization movement, he did not take dramatic actions to promote emancipation, he did not found the Haskalah movement, and he certainly did not lay the foundations for change in religious ritual. Yet for all these reservations, his historical importance to eighteenth-century European culture and the history of the Jews is self-evident. The story of his life gives expression to the dilemmas posed to the Jews by the "modern condition." His public standing demonstrates the possibility of emerging from a separate cultural existence; he exemplifies the rise of a modern Jewish intellectual elite no longer identical to the rabbinical elite, and not restricted in its knowledge to traditional religious sources. His thought marks the beginning of a liberal Jewish philosophy seeking to promote such values as the love of man, religious tolerance, and a multicultural society that interprets Judaism according to rationalistic and moral criteria.

But above all Mendelssohn's importance lies in his not having been a naïve representative of an Enlightenment that assumes a vital historical process culminating in triumph of reason, progress, and the happiness of humankind. Even as he embraced dreams of opportunities presented by modernity, he feared that Enlightenment might fail—a fear fed by his experiences as a Jew. Mendelssohn, the sober Jewish humanist of the eighteenth century, who even at the height of the public fame discerned the menacing "specters" of prejudice, coercion, and oppression, placed at the center of the Berlin Enlightenment, as a warning sign, his "humanistic imperative." The value of this warning, and of his humanistic message, can perhaps be appreciated fully only from the historical perspective that includes the tragic fate of European Jewry in the mid-twentieth century. If Mendelssohn could have predicted what was to happen to Jews in Berlin some 150 years after his death, he might well have shouted the words he muttered in anger, despair, and revulsion when he and his family were attacked by stone-throwing youths on Unter den Linden: "People, people, when will you stop this?"

CHRONOLOGY

1729   Moses Mendelssohn is born in Dessau.

1740   Friedrich II ("The Great") succeeds to the Prussian throne.
        Mendelssohn begins his studies with Rabbi David Fränkel.

1742   Maimonides' *The Guide for the Perplexed* is printed in Jessnitz.

1743   Mendelssohn comes to Berlin and resumes studies under Fränkel.

1750   The "general privilege" for the Jews of Prussia.
        Mendelssohn is engaged as a private tutor to the children of the Bernhard family.

1753   Mendelssohn is employed as a clerk in Bernhard's silk factory.
        Mendelssohn's friendship with Lessing begins.

1754   Lessing's play *Die Juden*, written in 1749, appears.

In the *Theatralische Bibliotek* journal Mendelssohn responds to Michaelis's criticism of Lessing.

1755   Mendelssohn publishes *Philosophischen Gespräche.*
Mendelssohn publishes *Über die Empfindungen.*
Together with Tobias Bock, Mendelssohn publishes *Kohelet Musar.*

1756   The Seven Years' War begins in Europe.
Lessing leaves Berlin.

1759   Voltaire publishes *Candide.*

1761   Mendelssohn travels to Hamburg and visits Rabbi Eybeschütz.
Mendelssohn publishes *Logical Terms.*
Mendelssohn meets Fromet Gugenheim and falls in love with her.
Mendelssohn is appointed manager of Bernhard's silk factory.
Mendelssohn's friendship with Thomas Abbt begins.

1762   Mendelssohn and Fromet Gugenheim are married.

1763   Mendelssohn is granted the status of *Schutzjude,* protected Jew, in Prussia.
Mendelssohn wins first prize in the Royal Academy of Science competition with his "On Evidence in Metaphysical Sciences."
Lavater visits Mendelssohn.
Mendelssohn is exempted from tax payment to the Berlin Jewish community.
The Seven Years' War ends.
The Mendelssohns' daughter Sarah is born.

1764   Sarah dies and another daughter, Brendel (who later takes the name Dorothea), is born.

1766   The Mendelssohns' son Chaim is born and dies.

1767   Mendelssohn publishes *Phädon.*
A daughter, Reikel, is born to the Mendelssohns.

1768   After Isaak Bernhard's death, Mendelssohn becomes a partner in his silk factory.

1769   The Lavater affair erupts.

A son, Mendel Abraham, is born to the Mendelssohns.
Mendelssohn publishes his commentary on
Ecclesiastes.

1770   Mendelssohn begins his German translation of the
Book of Psalms.
Mendelssohn writes his response to Lavater.
A son, Joseph, is born to the Mendelssohns.
Mendelssohn visits the crown prince of Braunschweig,
and visits Lessing at Wolfenbüttel.

1771   Mendelssohn is elected a fellow of the Royal Academy
of Science, but the king does not approve the election.
Mendelssohn is stricken by what is diagnosed as
mental stress.
The Berlin Jewish community appoints Mendelssohn
an elder of the community.
Mendelssohn visits Sanssouci palace and is received by
Baron von Fritsch of Saxony.

1772   Mendelssohn disagrees with Rabbi Emden in
correspondence about the Mecklenburg-Schwerin
affair of delayed burial.

1773   Mendelssohn first visits Bad Pyrmont.

1775   Lavater publishes his book on physiognomy
Mendel Mendelssohn dies at age six.
A daughter, Jente (Henriette), is born to the
Mendelssohns.
Mendelssohn intercedes on behalf of the Swiss Jewish
communities.

1776   A son, Abraham, is born to the Mendelssohns.
Mendelssohn travels to Dresden.

1777   Salomon Maimon comes to Germany.
Mendelssohn travels to Königsberg and meets Kant.
Mendelssohn intercedes on behalf of the Jews of
Dresden.

1778   Mendelssohn publishes a prospectus for the *Bi'ur*
project.
The *Hinukh Ne'arim* school is established in Berlin.

The Mendelssohns' daughter Sise is born and dies.

1779 Lessing writes his play *Nathan der Weise.*
Rabbi Raphael Kohen of Hamburg calls for the banning of the *Bi'ur.*
David Friedländer publishes *The Reader for Jewish Children.*
Herz Homberg is hired as the Mendelssohn children's private tutor.

1780 Publishing of the *Bi'ur* commences.

1781 Dohm publishes *Concerning the Amelioration of the Civil Status of the Jews.*
Emperor Joseph II promulgates the first of his Edicts of Tolerance.
Lessing dies.

1782 Wessely publishes *Divrei Shalom ve-Emet.*
Euchel founds the Society of Friends of the Hebrew Language.
Mendelssohn publishes his preface to Manasseh Ben Israel's *Vindiciae Judaeorum,* Vindication of the Jews.
Cranz publishes his *Das Forschen nach Licht und Recht* (The search for light and right).
A son, Nathan, is born to the Mendelssohns.

1783 Mendelssohn publishes *Jerusalem; or, On Religious Power and Judaism.*
Brendel Mendelssohn marries Simon Veit.
Mendelssohn is elected member of honor of the Wednesday Society.
Publication of *Ha'measef* commences in Königsberg.
The translation of the Book of Psalms is published.

1784 Mendelssohn and Kant engage the question "What Is Enlightenment?"
Hamann criticizes Mendelssohn.

1785 Jacobi foments the *Pantheismusstreit.*
Reikel Mendelssohn marries Mendel Meyer.

Mendelssohn publishes *Morgenstunden* (Morning hours).

Mendelssohn concludes *An die Freunde Lessings* (To Lessing's friends).

1786   Moses Mendelssohn dies on 4 January.

King Friedrich II dies on 17 August.

SELECT BIBLIOGRAPHY

Writings by Mendelssohn

Gesammelte Schriften, Jubiläumsausgabe. 24 vols. Stuttgart, 1971–2004.

Selections from His Writings. Ed. Eva Jospe. New York, 1975.

Jerusalem; or, On Religious Power and Judaism. Trans. Allan Arkush. Introduction and Commentary by Alexander Altmann. Hanover, 1983.

Philosophical Writings. Trans. and ed. Daniel O. Dahlstrom. Cambridge, 1997.

Jerusalem, oder über religiöse Macht und Judentum. Ed. David Martyn. Bielefeld, 2001.

The First English Biography and Translations. 3 vols. Ed. James Schmidt. Bristol, 2002.

Ausgewählte Werke, Studienausgabe. 2 vols. Darmstadt, 2009.

Biographies and Studies

Altmann, Alexander. *Moses Mendelssohn: A Biographical Study.* Philadelphia, 1973.

———. "Moses Mendelssohn as the Archetypal German Jew." In *The Jewish Response to German Culture*, ed. Jehuda Reinharz and Walter Schatzberg. Hanover, 1985. Pp. 17–31.

Arkush, Allan. *Moses Mendelssohn and the Enlightenment.* Albany, NY, 1994.

———. "The Questionable Judaism of Moses Mendelssohn." *New German Critique* 77 (1999): 29–44.

Behm, Britta L. *Moses Mendelssohn und die Transformation der jüdischen Erziehung in Berlin.* Munich, 2002.

Bourel, Dominique. *Moses Mendelssohn, la naissance du Judaisme moderne.* Paris, 2004.

Breuer, Edward. *The Limits of Enlightenment: Jews, Germans and the Eighteenth-century Study of Scripture.* Cambridge, Mass., 1996.

Euchel, Isaac. *Toldot rabbenu he-chacham Moshe ben Menachem* (The History of Our Master and Sage Moses ben Menachem). Berlin, 1788.

Feiner, Shmuel. *Haskalah and History: The Emergence of a Modern Jewish Historical Consciousness.* Oxford, 2002.

———. *The Jewish Enlightenment.* Philadelphia, 2004.

———. "Mendelssohn and Mendelssohn's Disciples: A Reexamination." *Year Book of the Leo Baeck Institute* 40 (1995): 133–167.

Feiner, Shmuel, and David Sorkin, eds. *New Perspectives on the Haskalah.* London, 2001.

Gillon, Meir. *Kohelet musar le-Mendelssohn al reka tekufato* (Mendelssohn's *Kohelet Musar* in Its Historical Context). Jerusalem, 1979.

Hess, Jonathan M. *Germans, Jews, and the Claims of Modernity.* New Haven, 2002.

Hilfrich, Carola. *Lebendige Schrift: Repräsentation und Idolatrie in Moses Mendelssohns Philosophie und Exegese des Judentums.* Munich, 2000.

Katz, Jacob. *Out of the Ghetto: The Social Background of Jewish Emancipation, 1770–1870.* Tel Aviv, 1985.

Kayserling, M. *Moses Mendelssohn, Sein Leben und Wirken.* Leipzig, 1888.

Knobloch, Heinz. *Herr Moses in Berlin, Auf den Spuren eines Menschenfreundes.* Frankfurt am Main, 1996.

Lowenstein, Steven. *The Berlin Jewish Community: Enlightenment, Family, and Crisis, 1770–1830.* Oxford, 1994.

———. "The Readership of Mendelssohn's Bible Translation." *Hebrew Union College Annual* 52 (1982): 179–213.

Meyer, Hermann. *Moses Mendelssohn Biographie.* Berlin, 1965.

Meyer, Michael A. *The Origins of the Modern Jew: Jewish Identity and European Culture in Germany, 1749–1824.* Detroit, 1979.

Schmidt, James. "The Question of the Enlightenment: Kant, Mendelssohn, and the *Mittwochgesellschaft,*" *Journal of the History of Ideas* 50 (1989): 269–291.

Schulte, Christoph. *Die jüdische Aufklärung, Philosophie, Religion, Geschichte.* Munich, 2002.

Sorkin, David. *The Berlin Haskalah and German Religious Thought: Orphans of Knowledge.* London, 2000.

———. "The Mendelssohn Myth and Its Method." *New German Critique* 77 (1999): 7–28.

———. *Moses Mendelssohn and the Religious Enlightenment.* London, 1996.

———. *The Transformation of German Jewry, 1780–1840.* New York, 1987.

Sutcliffe, Adam. *Judaism and the Enlightenment.* Cambridge, 2003.

INDEX

Note: The abbreviation MM in subheadings refers to Moses Mendelssohn.